# LIVE IN THE
# POWER ZONE

## KIRK CHARLES

### PZ PUBLISHING

This publication is designed to provide accurate and authoritative information in regard to the subject matter covered. It is sold with the understanding that the publisher is not engaged in rendering legal, accounting or other professional service. If legal advice or other expert assistance is required, the services of a competent professional person should be sought.

Library of Congress Cataloging-in-Publication Data

ISBN: 0-9836080-0-8

ISBN-13: 978-0-9836080-0-4

Printed in the United States of America

This book is dedicated to
The Man & Woman Upstairs
Who continue to
Whisper in my ear and
Guide my every step
When I stumble and
Lose my way.

# CONTENTS

# A Note from the Author

Dear Reader,

This book is a labor of love which entered my consciousness about twenty years ago. It contains original thoughts and ideas, as well as pearls of wisdom from those who have inspired me through bold words and courageous actions.

What makes this endeavor most interesting and a little scary—*or dare I say exciting*—is that it is unedited. I was advised quite some time ago that everyone needs an editor, which I believe is true. But, when it came time to bring my thoughts to words on paper, I didn't have the cash to pay for professional editing services. However, my woefully thin wallet turned out to be a blessing in disguise. It challenged me to be daring and overcome my fear of putting my dream into the public domain. Needless to say, lack of money wasn't going to stop my show!

My paltry financial resources also caused me to think *why water down my thoughts with editing?* As a consequence, what you have before you is unfiltered, undiluted and straight from the heart. Simply put, I'm steppin' out on faith and givin' you all I've got.

With that in mind you will soon discover there is no particular writing style and rules of grammar are often tossed to the wind for the vernacular to take root. It's all about you and me having a casual conversation and telling it like it is, as we explore the limitless possibilities before you. The end result is pure passion on paper. My only wish is that propels you to live a life of bliss!

May you forever Live in the Power Zone,

*Kirk Charles*

# INTRODUCTION

*B*eyond a shadow of a doubt, right now is the most precious moment of your life. Decisions need to be made, actions must be taken, and tick-tock goes the clock. There are many reasons why this moment is so meaningful, but for now we need only concern ourselves with a few. First and most obvious, this is the only moment you have. You've spent the past and you can't borrow against the future. Clearly that makes this present moment your most valuable commodity. Second, you have the power to stride forward. By no means are you stuck in the mud. If you're audacious enough to take the first step and let positive momentum kick in, who knows what will happen. And last, you have the ability to change direction. If you're traveling on a dusty, winding road to nowhere, all you have to do is make a few left and right turns. Before you know it you'll be riding high on the adventure of your life. With those points in mind, how you handle this moment—the *here* and *now*—will make or break your future.

To maximize on the here and now it's in your best interest to use the past as a learning tool to be invested for future gain. If you do so and you throw into the mix some serious sweat equity, critical questions will be asked of you. The answers you give will be heavily scrutinized—*by life itself*—in light of the frantic social and economic whirlpools we're all spinning in. At this point your best chance to live the life you desire is to be brutally honest with the person staring at you in the mirror when answering those questions. If you are willing to open up and do that, life will present you with unimaginable opportunities for growth and advancement. And, if you are courageous enough to take advantage of those opportunities, you will also experience an unbelievable adrenaline rush that will empower you—*and that's when the fun begins.*

To turn opportunity into a bright and exciting future, all you must do is one simple thing: *live in the power zone.* Quite frankly it's what you were meant to do. However, to do so, you must venture into the unknown. A power zone existence isn't for the faint of heart. It's reserved for those who are willing to buck the odds, disregard the naysayers and go for it. And, if you don't feel you have any power, it's most likely bottled up deep inside your soul waiting for you to pull the cork. Admittedly you must be extraordinarily brave to uncork it because the forces against you are sinister. You can best believe you will be attacked from every conceivable angle if there's the slightest hint that you're taking advantage of your power in order to live a higher quality life. With that in the forefront of your consciousness, it's now time to tackle some of the toughest questions of your life.

*Are you prepared to handle the challenges life will present to you?* Obviously that's a difficult question to start with because there's no certainty regarding what's going to be thrown your way. Yet you surely know by now that preparation on purpose is essential to rise to the occasion. Without it your life will be entangled in a web of chaos and confusion and there's the potential for some really ugly situations to start brewing. In the 1960's *The Temptations* harmoniously sang *get ready 'cause here I come.* Without doubt life is comin' at 'cha with some serious challenges and you can easily maneuver around most of the ugliness by simply being ready.

Maybe it's best to take a peek at a few other questions before answering the first one. You need to know exactly where your mentality is regarding preparedness. Check out the following *10 Power Questions for Preparation...*

- *Will you forgive yourself for the ugly mistakes you've made?*
- *Will you liberate your soul from haunting regrets?*
- *Will you turn your back on a life of mediocrity?*
- *Will you plan for the future?*
- *Will you open your mind to unlimited possibilities?*
- *Will you maximize on opportunity?*
- *Will you give before expecting to receive?*
- *Will you work hard before playing hard?*
- *Will you share your wealth of knowledge?*
- *Will you refuse to give up?*

And a bonus question...

- *Will you make the personal sacrifices necessary to guarantee a lifetime of success after success?*

As you can see there's a whole lot to think about. However, if you can answer at least half of those questions in the affirmative, *The Temptations* would be extremely proud of you because you're definitely ready. You've got a great shot at overcoming any challenge life may throw your way.

The real deal is that an abundance of character, confidence and courage is required to overcome the *external* and *internal* forces against you. By the nature of the previous questions it should be clearly understood that 95% of the forces against you are internal. Believe it or not, the enemy ain't outside, it's inside. Ultimately, to combat that insidious 95%, you must make some major personal sacrifices. Those sacrifices will most likely include a lot of time, a lot of money and a lot of heartache—*and definitely sacrificing any excuses you may have used in the past that pinned you down and defeated you.* Without the willingness to sacrifice there's absolutely no other way to succeed and realize your full potential.

As a general rule, in this world you must give something to get something. You've got to put some skin in the game, otherwise fuggedaboutit—*you don't stand a chance.* If you can't accept that rule put this book down and pick up the latest romance novel. Freebees are a rarity that only the average person expects, so if you wanna play you gotta pay the price. With that understanding, if you're ready, willing and able to move onward and upward, this book was conceived and written especially for you so you may find true bliss. The only way to do that is to be able to deliver when everything is on the line—*and it is.*

Your dreams and aspirations are hanging in the balance. *It's crunch time!*

There's a story about the legendary Sugar Ray Robinson, the greatest pound-for-pound prizefighter of all time. He had superlative technique and prowess, matched with unbelievable power and grace. His lightening quick speed and uncanny timing was combined with flair and charisma. He had it all—*he was the complete package.* And, to top it off, he was a handsome devil. He could have jumped out of the boxing ring and onto the movie screen. Lucky for us we were blessed to see him embrace his talent and work magic as a prizefighter.

As fluid and rhythmic as he was in the heat of battle, Sugar was having a lackluster day in the ring during a training camp session. He was preparing for another major prizefight and the fire just wasn't there. Under normal circumstances he had knock-out power in both hands, but for some reason he just didn't have that pop in his punch. As his trainer watched him pitifully go through the motions, he became more and more frustrated and incensed. Finally his trainer couldn't take it anymore and he snapped. He jumped up, yanked Sugar out of the ring and dragged him into the far corner of the gym.

He then whispered something in Sugar's ear, which no one else heard. To this day what was said is a mystery, but whatever it was it inspired Sugar and motivated him. Sugar then jumped back into the ring and he was on fire. His trainer knew the exact combination of buttons to press to elevate Sugar into his *power zone.* Instead of laying back and hesitating, Sugar took the initiative and made things happen. The pop was back in his punch and, once again, he was as sweet as sugar. That's why, when we talk about Sugar Ray Robinson, we talk about a legend.

Let's pretend you are Sugar Ray Robinson or whoever your model of excellence is. You can be Bill Gates, Barack Obama, Barbara Walters, Warren Buffet, Beyoncé, the Dalai Lama, Superman—*or you can just be yourself.* One goal of this book is to be your coach so that lifeless pages will vivify and whisper sweet nothings of inspiration and success in your ear. Be prepared, because it's very likely you'll hear exactly what you need to hear to turn you on so you may do battle in the ring of life. Then, instead of worrying about being knocked out, your passions will flare and you'll have the intensity and drive to deliver the knockout blow. And forget about laying back and hesitating—*those days are over!* There's no earthly reason why you can't catch fire, just like

Sugar Ray. You may not be a world class prizefighter, but you can be a champion, when you find your power zone.

So, what is the *power zone*? It's simply a higher range of personal performance and creativity. It's a stratum where you are most efficient and most effective. Simply put, it's when you are at your best. If we use a scale of 1 to 10—with 1 on the low end and 10 on the high end—obviously we all want to operate at level 10. Being human we can't hit a perfect 10 all the time, it just ain't happenin'. However, the question is what if you could vacillate between levels 8 through 10 on a consistent basis? And, if you had a bad day, what if you only fell to level 7 instead of plummeting to level 1 or 2? Maybe it sounds like a far stretch, but many people are reaching for the stars and making it happen. They're shooting for perfection and every so often they hit it. And, when they miss perfection, as they most likely will, they don't pitifully fall to pieces. At the very least they continue to execute, with maximum effort, and land on excellence. Levels 7 through 10 comprise their domain of performance and creativity. Essentially they've discovered how to *live in the power zone.*

Following are descriptions of the levels of performance and creativity. At any given point in time, regarding the activity you're engaged in, you're most likely operating at one of the following levels...

1. **Repugnance.** Stop rollin' in the gutter. You're offending yourself and those who may care about you. At this lowest level it's hopeless, so move on to something else.

2. **Nauseation.** Stop fakin' the funk, it's sickening. You're making people regurgitate. It's time to get serious and man up. There is hope for you.

3. **Apathy.** Stop pretending to care. Everybody can see your heart is not in it. You've gotta give a doggone about something.

4. **Mediocrity.** You can survive at this level, but who would want to? It's a tasteless and boring way of life.

5. **Average.** Anybody can do the average thing, so now is the time to aim higher. If you're not careful you'll slip down into the abyss of the lower levels.

6. **Comfort.** Okay, so you're better than average, so what? That ain't sayin' much at all. There's a fine line between comfort and laziness, so be on guard.

7. **Excellence.** You're doin' well, you're happy, you're pleased with your progress, you're in charge. But, you know you have much more to give. Start givin' it up!

8. **Exceptionalism.** Now we're talkin'. Here is where the real action begins. You're thriving in the game, you're making things happen and you're head and shoulders above the rest. Do your thing!

9. **Supremacy.** You got it goin' on, you know it and so does everyone else. You're rubbin' elbows with the movers and shakers and hobnobbin' your way to the stratosphere. You're the best of the best. How sweet it is!

10. **Perfection.** What can you say? You're firing on all cylinders. You're in complete harmony with your creative genius. You can't explain how or why everything is going your way, nor

do you know how long it's going to last, so kick back and enjoy the ride!

Levels 1 through 3 comprise the *danger zone* and are to be avoided at all costs. Far too many are wallowing in the *danger zone* and don't realize the consequences. It's a sad existence. Levels 4 through 6 comprise the *ordinary zone* and it's where the majority of people operate. It's a bland way of life with little to no sparks of excitement. As aforementioned levels 7 through 10 comprise the *power zone*. It's where all the action is and where the magic happens. Most important, it can be your playground!

How do the zones of performance and creativity factor into your life? First, you have to decide who you want to be. For example, when I conduct personal training sessions I often ask my clients, *"Do you want to be Joe-2 or Joe-8?"* Or I may ask, *"Are you committed to turning Joanne-3 into Joanne-9?"* And for the bold and adventurous, *"You're not satisfied with Bobby-6 when Bobby-10 is waiting for you in the power zone, are you?"* Ninety-nine percent of my clients desire a *power zone* existence regarding health and physical fitness. They are willing to do what it takes to climb out of the ignominy of the *danger zone* and doldrums of the *ordinary zone* because they have the option and willpower to do so.

Regarding business professionals I may consult with, many are in sales with commission based salaries. Without question extraordinary mental puissance is required for them to hit sales quotas and make the cut each and every quarter. But, for some reason, some fall off track and don't make the necessary phone calls, nor do they follow up on their leads. They start coming into the office later and later each month and take way too many evenings off. Many who were once at level 7 or above got a little too comfortable and slipped into the *ordinary zone* before the alarm bells clamored.

For those in sales you've gotta stay on top of your game. You know what you must do to rise from the dust—make calls, book appointments, conduct presentations and close deals. Your heart and soul must be invested in every moment. It ain't rocket science, it's just hard work. If you do the right things you'll elevate back to level 7. And, with true desire and patience, you may even rise to levels 8 through 10 and *live in the power zone*. It's all about commitment.

Reality dictates that it's difficult or even impossible to operate in the *power zone* in everything that you do, so pick your battles wisely. You may be great in one area and poor in another, so the *power zone* only need apply to what is essential or desirable for your wellbeing. The question is: *Are you living in the power zone regarding what's important to you?* Let's say you're a great business executive, but a poor golfer. That's fine as long as your business is thriving and you're not trying to make the cut on the PGA tour. Maybe you're a great parent, but a poor long distance runner. As long as your kids are happy and thriving, and you're not competing in the Olympic Games, everything is cool. As I've heard the late, great business philosopher Jim Rohn warn many times, *"Don't major in minor things."* Shoot for the *power zone* regarding what's important and don't fret about what's not. Sadly many people don't know the difference which is why most are writhing in the *ordinary zone* and teetering in the *danger zone.*

Obviously determining what is important is a highly personal proposition which may require much introspection. Your values and ideals will come into play and it's advisable not to compromise them too much, if at all. Sometimes you gotta stick to your guns to be comfortable in your own skin. It's easy to see how the 10 levels can apply to many aspects of your life, but there are three critical areas you may want to hone in on: health, relationships and career. In those areas it's best to *live in the power zone* and give it all you've got. Beyond those areas, if your performance or level of creativity is at a subpar level, it's probably inconsequential as long as it doesn't make you uncomfortable. And since we're all unique, everyone's *power zone* is different. Your level 6 might be another person's level 8, so don't be overly concerned about comparing yourself to others or some generic standard. Being you and using your own scale is your best bet to flourish and soar.

Maybe you have always felt that you have something magnificent and powerful inside, dying to burst out and flourish. Like many you may not even know what it is, but since it resonates deeply in your soul, you've been relentlessly driven to search, question, think, create and dream. Undoubtedly, if you simply keep on doing what you're doing, sooner or later the sky will open up and the sun will shine brightly. It's purely a matter of time. But, the most excruciating thing is sitting on life's runway and waiting. You're fueled up and ready to go, but something is stopping you dead in your tracks.

Whatever it may be, the tables have now turned in your favor. If you focus you'll clearly see that you're getting a green light, directly from Air Traffic Control, that *now is the time to take off.* You've got to get a grip and recognize it's your turn to fly high in the friendly sky. Any hesitation will turn into devastation.

Many people don't take off and fly because of closed minds and hardened attitudes—*let that not be you.* Open your mind like a flower when the sun comes up and soak in all the information in these pages, without bias. The key is to be receptive to unlimited possibility. Martha Stewart, business magnate, television show host and author believes, *"Without an open-minded mind, you can never be a great success."* Something tells me she knows what she's talkin' about. If you're brave enough to invite new ideas and new trains of thought, there's no telling what you can do, achieve and become. Before you know it you'll be taking off, your dreams will begin to materialize and you'll wonder why life is so grand.

As pop icon Seal would sing, *Bring It On.* It's time to *Live in the Power Zone!*

# THE
# DYNAMIC DESTINY
# PRINCIPLE

Venture to Dream
with passionate Desire,
Make unwavering Decisions
with faithful Devotion,
Maintain fearless Determination
with obedient Discipline,
And, above all, be Daring,
Then behold Deliverance
of your Dynamic Destiny.

*he Dynamic Destiny Principle* is the foundation of *Live in the Power Zone.* To use it effectively and ensure we're taking off in the right direction, we must first come to a meeting of the minds. From this point forward it's in your best interest to recognize and embrace one simple fact: *you are a winner.* If you think you're not, you're gravely mistaken. Maybe you didn't get the memo, but it's crystal clear that you are a winner simply because you're committing valuable time and energy into reading this book. You're focused and you're craving mental nourishment, as you allow the information in these pages to pour into your mind. And to top it off, like cream, you expect to rise to the top with the information you receive.

The real deal is that winners are *willing* to focus and digest when valuable information is tossed their way. Their dominant modality is to listen and learn even when they appear to be relaxing and having fun. Consequently, they use their eyes and ears much more than their mouths. Through extraordinary self-control they resist any temptation to drown others out by babbling inane and useless words. Winners are continually developing their auditory and visual senses which keep them fixated on self-improvement and self-mastery. They absorb information like a sponge and have an insatiable appetite for knowledge. Most important, winners use information and knowledge they receive to be proactive instead of reactive. As a result negative things usually don't happen to them because they're making positive things happen for them. It must be clearly understood that the willingness to focus and digest, combined with the desire to listen and learn, gives winners the *winning edge* for success. If for no other reason than your commitment to read further, you must embrace the fact that *you are a winner.*

Now that you know what you are, we can journey into *The Dynamic Destiny Principle* by first defining the word *dynamic.* The dictionary says dynamic is *something related to physical force; something marked by continuous, productive, activity or change;* and, also, *something marked by energy.* Those meanings bring to mind someone who is always on the move; someone who creates; someone who causes powerful and positive things to happen; and someone who is relentless in pursuit of excellence.

Oprah Winfrey is a prime example of a dynamic human being in motion. She started out as a poor and abused child. Her abject circumstances could have killed the spirit of the average young lady, but she had big dreams. Because of her relentless pursuit of excellence, she now has the best and most successful talk show in TV history and everyone wants to be on it—*including yours truly*. When someone has written a book and is on her show, overnight the book is a success. She has her own magazine, her own movie production company, she's an actress—*it seems like there's nuthin' she can't do*. And if that's not enough, she founded OWN, her own cable TV network. Oprah is philanthropic and donates money to many different causes to make the world a better place. There's no doubt about it, she is the essence of dynamism. And, in the course of all that, she's managed to rise from obscurity to attain billionaire status, which ain't easy. She's found her *power zone* and it's a joy to see her in action.

There's something even more important about being dynamic. There's a superior mental attitude that dynamic people like Oprah have that is a salient part of their DNA. As a result unbelievable thoughts are firing off in the dynamic person's mind like firecrackers. Those thoughts allow him or her to be mentally liberated and take on challenge after challenge. They inspire a dynamic person to always be thinking *wow, I can do it...I'm going to make it happen!* To be perfectly clear, dynamic people like Oprah are not wondering *can I make it happen.* They flew past that checkpoint eons ago. Dynamic human beings have graduated to declaring *I'm going to make it happen!* It's a distinction that must be crystal clear in your mind to *live in the power zone.* Oprah knows what she has deep, down inside and she knows how to let it flow. With that type of mental disposition it's no wonder why she is the undisputed queen of television.

Next we must define *destiny*, arguably the most perplexing concept since the beginning of time. Destiny is defined as *a predetermined future that can't be altered or changed.* It means certain things are bound to happen and there's nothing you can do about it. To be honest, that definition, on face value, appears to be woefully weak. It implies that you have no influence over your future. Taken to the extreme, essentially you're impotent and you're just going through the motions of life. Does that make any sense at all? If that's true there appears to be no need to find your *power zone* and take on life's challenges; therefore, we're not going to buy into that definition. We can't afford to waste the precious moments we have on this earth with a concept so disempowering.

From this point forward let's be proactive and redefine destiny for empowerment. Our new definition for destiny now will be *a future over which you have unlimited influence.* Please note our new and empowering definition does not say you can *control* your destiny. Control is reserved for a higher power, so we don't want to mess with that. Being a mere mortal it's greatly advisable to wield your *influence* instead of attempting to control. To control means to dominate or command, while influence means the power to sway or direct. Through swaying and directing you can set a series of events in motion with the purpose and expectation of producing a desired outcome. The late, great Congressman Adam Clayton Powell, Jr. gave a speech entitled *What's In Your Hand?* If it wasn't clear before, now you know the answer—*the power to influence your destiny.* The real question is *are you able to tap into your power of influence?* With that question in mind, our empowering definition of destiny is based on a quote whose source is questionable, yet whose wisdom in boundless...

*If you sow a thought, you reap an action...*
*If you sow an action, you reap a habit...*
*If you sow a habit, you reap a character...*
*If you sow a character, you reap a destiny.*

The bottom line is there is only one thing over which you have control: *how you use your mind.* Of course, to a great extent how you use your mind is based on what is in it. If you have self-defeating garbage bouncing around in your head, it's a challenge to get out of bed in the morning. However, when there's a consistent flow of positive and inspiring information exciting and igniting your consciousness, all types of adventures may be sparked. Unequivocally, controlling what and how you think will influence your destiny. American writer and entrepreneur Orison Marden believed...

*Our destiny changes with our thought; we shall become what we wish to become, and do what we wish to do, when our habitual thought corresponds with our desire.*

More simply put, the secret of Napoleon Hill's classic book *Think & Grow Rich* is six little words: *we become what we think about.*

When someone mentions the word destiny Itzhak Perlman immediately pops into my mind, one of the great music virtuosi of our time. Itzhak was born in Palestine in 1945. At the age of three he heard a classical music concert on the radio and it was clear he was destined to be a violinist. He began taking violin lessons; however, in 1949 the unthinkable happened. At the precious age of four he contracted polio and lost the use of his legs. As devastating as that was, his passion for music blossomed. He continued to pour his heart and soul into his violin by practicing religiously.

In 1958, at the age of 13, Itzhak was brought to New York City by the *Ed Sullivan Show* for two performances. His display of talent made him a shining star in America. At 18 years of age he made his professional debut at Carnegie Hall. On the 4th of July in 1986 he was honored with the Medal of Liberty by President Ronald Reagan. Itzhak collaborated with composer John Williams to create the musical score for *Schindler's List*, which won the Academy Award in 1993. During all of that time, and to this day, Itzhak tours the world and has generously donated his time and money to worthy causes. Lucky for me I was able to catch one of his many superlative performances. I remember him walking on stage with two canes for support. Then he sat down, put his violin in its proper place, and created musical magic. It was incredible.

When you look as Itzhak's life being struck by polio may have been the determining factor in the discovery of his musical genius. If he didn't have polio maybe he wouldn't have practiced so diligently, instead opting for some other activity. Who knows, maybe he would have canned the violin altogether and occupied his time doing other things. All that considered, it appears as though he was *destined* to be a master violinist—*or was he?*

What really happened is that Itzhak *influenced* and *created* his destiny through resolution and devotion to his craft. Regardless of his circumstances and any raw talent he may have had, he still had to put in the hard labor to attain his lofty status. Obviously he could have wallowed in self-pity because of his physical condition, but he decided to rise to the occasion and overcome any obstacles in front of him. There's no doubt that it's impossible to ascend to his level in any other way. Polio or no polio, he made it happen through hard work and sacrifice. Deservedly so, he's considered one of the all time masters of the violin.

When we marry the words dynamic and destiny the *Dynamic Destiny Principle* is given birth: *How to realize a vibrant and exciting future which is influenced and brought to life by how you use your mind.* It's just that simple and it ain't rocket science. It's as if you're a tennis player and your opponent hits the ball over the net to you. You know you can hit the ball back over the net, with power and grace; and it's your choice of how you want to hit the ball. You can hit it high, low, with spin, etcetera. The ball is in your court and through some God-given power you can return it wherever and however you want to. It's the same with your mind. Information is being hit over the net into your mind for you to think about. You have the God-given power to return that information to the universe in the form of *influence*. If you do so, with conviction, it's quite possible you will bring to life a scintillating future.

As we venture further through these pages what we'll discover is how certain individuals live life to its fullest; how they take advantage of all that life has to offer; how they maintain prosperity and inner peace; and how they develop into champions. If you've wandered into a pit of quicksand attempting to achieve those objectives, there's no need to sink any further. The *Dynamic Destiny Principle* is now at your fingertips.

Your mission—*should you choose to accept it*—is to do whatever it takes to get the job done, just like Oprah and Itzhak. They're not extraordinary individuals; they're just like you and me. What has distinguished them is that they've made extraordinary use of their minds. They've adopted *winning attitudes* by letting *winning thoughts* dominate their mentalities. You can do that too! Understand that realizing your Dynamic Destiny is not an episode of *Mission Impossible*. We're dealing with real life where your dreams can and will come true, if you put in the effort and pay your dues.

*The Dynamic Destiny Principle* is based on very simple ideas, some or all of which will easily fit into your life plan. And, by the way, if you don't have a life plan, don't let that or anything else stop you from moving forward. As we continue on your excitement and enthusiasm will build momentum and motivate you to devise a plan. Before you know it you will put those positive emotions into motion and reap the benefits of them. The powerful concepts of the *Dynamic Destiny Principle* are Dreaming, Desire, Decisions, Devotion,

Determination, Discipline, Daring and Deliverance. Maybe all eight will be in your plan or maybe just one—*whatever it takes to catapult you to a higher level!*

As you can see the eight concepts are nothing new, they're simply solid fundamentals upon which to build a successful life. My great-grandmother would often tell me, *"Boy, there ain't nuthin' new under the sun."* With her wisdom in tow, we're simply going to view the eight concepts from a different vantage point. If you're willing to do that, you will benefit from new and empowering perspectives on your experiences and aspirations. All we need to do is turn on certain lights in your mind so we can maneuver with confidence.

Imagine being in an unfamiliar environment with unfamiliar people. Suddenly, boom, the lights go out and there's total darkness. People stop moving, stop talking and there's deafening silence. Undoubtedly the comfort everyone felt when the lights were on instantly turns to discomfort, maybe even anxiety. Some people stay cool and calm but, as usual, somebody always starts to freak out under the stress. And, if the lights stay off for too long, complete chaos will take over. But, suddenly, for no apparent reason, the lights come back on and everybody is comfortable again. People start mingling, talking, laughing and order is immediately restored because people can see clearly in the light. The correlation is that for many of us the light in our minds is dim or there is total darkness. Unfortunately the lack of sufficient light is the perfect breeding ground for confusion and anxiety. As they continue to fester chaos puts a vice-grip on your life. Even worse, for some of us there's a bigger problem: *the light is out and there is no electricity to turn it on.*

There are two goals you will be able to attain using the *Dynamic Destiny Principle.* First, we have to generate some electricity and get the juices flowing. Second, we have to be courageous and pull the switch to turn on the light. Think of the electricity as passion and the light as clarity. The bottom line is once we turn the lights on mental chaos will be chased away and mental clarity will be at the foundation of our actions. Then something very interesting and exciting happens—*we can turn possibility into probability.*

There have been about a zillion and one books written over the last few years about possibility thinking, simply because what can possibly happen is intriguing. In fact, the possibilities of life are limitless. We all know anything can happen, but the question is *what* will happen? Sure, anything is possible, but is it *probable*? And most important, what is the likelihood that what we want to happen will happen?

With those questions in mind is seems as though talking about possibility is meaningless unless we infuse probability into the discussion. For example, let's say you are offered a trillion dollars to jump from the $100^{th}$ floor of a high rise building. There is a *possibility* you could survive. The chances may be slim to none and what condition you'd be in upon landing, who knows? But, since the *probability* of survival is one in a billion at best, would you be optimistic enough to give it your best shot? Something tells me you'd decline the offer because the risk-reward ratio is completely out of whack. Obviously studying possibility is a necessary activity, but studying *probability* will make all the difference in the world. Without doubt it will be the difference between life and death of your *Dynamic Destiny*.

The real deal is when you work on turning possibility into probability you can tweak the odds of living a successful life in your favor. As you work on doing that what you'll find is that you have a new direction which entices you; a new perspective which excites you; and a new sense of confidence which motivates you to become a champion.  More important than all of that, your spirit will be revived and set free, which is really what life is all about.  At that point who knows what incredible things might happen.

American essayist and poet Ralph Waldo Emerson had an interesting philosophy...

> *We must trust the perfection of the creation so far as to believe that whatever curiosity the order of things has awakened in our minds, the order of things can satisfy.*

The beauty and gifts you have deep, down inside your soul were planted there for a reason.  You may never know why, but does it really matter?  As my favorite business philosopher Jim Rohn would say...

> *Some people are always studying the roots while others are picking the fruit.  It depends on which end of it you want to be on.*

As your mind awakens you'll see there's no intelligent rationale to fight against what you have been blessed with. My best advice is to simply work with it and take it to the highest level possible. You're more than welcome to use the *Dynamic Destiny Principle* to enjoy the process as you *Live in the Power Zone!*

# Dream

*When was the last time you had a dream and you took action on it?*

*There have been many books written about unrealized dreams, all because someone didn't take action. It's time to wake up out of the dream and do the right thing.*

*W*e could write a million books about the dreams people have let slip through their fingers. The bottom line is there's nothing like the power of a vivid dream, but that power will only vivify if you take action on it. The great poet Henry David Thoreau believed...

> *If one advances confidently in the direction of his dreams, and endeavors to live the life which he has imagined, he will meet with a success unexpected in common hours.*

The key word from Thoreau's pen is *advances.* That's what dreaming is really all about. Without advancement a dream quickly melts into a murky pool of delusion.

When I think of dreaming I remember jogging through the park with my wife, one fine summer afternoon. As we stopped for a break we watched some young kids playing Little League baseball. There was one little guy on the batter's deck, Johnny, waiting for his turn at bat. As most hitters do, he was warming up by swinging his bat back and forth. Then he picked up another bat so he could swing two and loosen up even more. As everyone could see, Johnny looked like a pro as he mesmerized the crowd.

It was the final inning and Johnny's team was down one run, so everybody was depending on him to deliver. He confidently strode into the batter's box, dug in with his cleats and prepared himself for battle. Johnny swung at the first pitch and missed—*strike one*. He then swung at the second pitch, a bad pitch in the dirt—*strike two*. He then backed out of the batter's box, composed himself, and stepped back in. The third pitch he jumped all over and smacked it right over the shortstop's head into the left field gap. As Johnny dashed toward first base you could tell he was going to stretch out a double, there was absolutely no doubt about it.

After Johnny rounded first base the left fielder threw the ball into second base. It was clear to everybody that Johnny would be thrown out, but Johnny was dead serious. He was giving it everything he had to get to second base. Johnny made a beautiful slide into second as the shortstop made the tag, but the second base umpire hesitated before he called him safe or out. The crowd waited with bated breath to see if Johnny would be a hero or a scapegoat. Finally, after what seemed like an eternity, the umpire signaled safe. The parents in the stands and the players on the bench went absolutely wild. If you didn't know any better, you may have thought it was the World Series. Johnny was pumped up—*he was on fire.* Since that time I've never seen a kid that excited. Then my wife made a comment I'll never forget. She said, *"Look at him, look at Johnny. He thinks he's in the Major Leagues!"*

As we continued jogging home I thought about that little guy, looking and acting like a pro. Then something hit me. I remembered a time when I was a kid his age, doing the same thing he was doing and feeling the same way he was feeling, like I was in the Major Leagues. And you know what, at that moment in time, I *was* in the Major Leagues. My mind was there, my body was there, my spirit was there—*I was there.* No one could tell me differently. The feeling was real because I didn't know the difference. When you're a kid life is surreal because you don't always know reality from fantasy. The beauty of that surreal existence is *you don't know what you cannot do*, which opens the door to endless possibilities. It's an unbelievably powerful state of mind, if it's focused in the right direction.

At Johnny's age, nine or ten years old, most kids don't have a realistic concept of the ups and downs of life. They don't understand relationships, earning a living or the bleak odds of breaking into Major League Baseball, unless they live in extraordinary circumstances. That being the case, as a kid your mind is free, clear and unobstructed. Kids aren't crippled by the self-imposed mental roadblocks adults have erected for themselves; as a result, their dreams are unfiltered and undiluted. They're also animated and potent, that's why being a kid can be so much fun. Johnny was in the moment—*he was in the zone.* There were fans in the stands cheering him on and he had the look and swagger of a professional. It was Major League Baseball personified and he was living his dream.

Then something else hit me. As we grow older for many of us something sublime and devastating happens: we realize the world isn't what we initially thought it was and we become disappointed. The feeling is similar to the letdown you may have experienced the moment you found out Santa Claus wasn't real. After we experience more and more letdowns our minds become tainted by reality. Our world starts to lose its color and you get the feeling that something is missing—*something just doesn't feel right*. Our dreams become distorted and lifeless and we start to manifest disbelief and self-doubt. What's really happening is that one by one our dreams and aspirations dry up like a puddle on a hot summer day and we're not even conscious of it. It's so different from the time when our minds were young, fertile and unblemished, filled with the seeds of dreams and infinite possibility. Question: *What happened and where did we get derailed?*

Of course, you know what happens next—*you stop dreaming*. Like a true cynic you believe dreaming is only for children. You begin to settle for the things you have as you try to put out of your mind the things you really, truly want. You just stop thinking about them and worry about staggering through one more dreadful day. Then, over time, you become bitter. Your attitude sours and life is a bland aftertaste, now that you realize your dreams will never come true.

Next question: *Who is to blame?* Somebody has to be the fall guy and take the heat, right? Or maybe it's nobody's fault and fate just dealt you a sorry hand. However, the real tragedy is when you're unable to play the hand you're dealt, regardless of how good or bad it may appear to be. You're at the card table staring at it, completely befuddled, wishing the cards would magically change—*but it ain't happening.* You get frustrated, throw it in, cash in your chips and get out of the game. As a result you get to stand on the sidelines and pout while everybody else has all the fun. It's a sad scenario, but that's how some people chose to live their lives. They are living in the *ordinary zone* or *danger zone* and they don't even know it. But, of course, that doesn't have to be you.

For some of us life really stinks all due to a lack of understanding regarding what a dream really is. A dream is not a delusion. Delusions can't come true, but dreams do. A dream is not a scenario that begins with the hopeless and hapless phrases *I wish I had...I wish I could...I wish I was...* That's not what it's about. A dream is not coveting someone's success, wishing it was yours. These are things we've all done, but now is the time to turn it all around.

What is a dream? A dream is a scenario that is *possible* and *probable* if you believe it, if you feel it and if you act on it. To break it down, let's look at the power of *belief.* When you believe in your dream it becomes your mental reality. It infuses a vision in your mind of the ideal situation for you. Sometimes your personal ideal is actually surreal, so be careful. For instance, dreaming that you're a super-cop who can run into a barrage of bullets can be a little dangerous. In Hollywood it always seems to work out, but in real life it ain't too pretty. Obviously your mental reality must be realistic. Your belief must encompass something you can actually see yourself doing, which is humanly possible, while keeping in mind seeing is believing.

Let's say you've dreamed of purchasing a brand new Lamborghini. It's certainly believable that you can purchase it, based on the thickness of your wallet. You can *see* it because you have a huge poster of it on your wall that reminds you of it every day. It's possible you can have it and, if you play your cards right, it will definitely become probable that you will get it.

The second part of dreaming is *feeling*. That little guy, Johnny, playing Little League baseball could feel his dream. He had on his uniform and he was swinging his bat. There was a huge crowd cheering him on and he was flying high without a care in the world. Feeling your dream is like seeing and believing it, and then stepping into it. Going back to that Lamborghini, it's believable that you can purchase it, but the next step is to test drive it so you can *feel* it. You want to feel the purr of the engine when you start it up and gently tap on the accelerator. Then you get on the highway and let it loose so you can feel the propulsion of the engine as you whiz by mortal cars. There's probably nothing in the world quite like it.

The last part of dreaming is *action*. You've actually got to *do* something. Some people *make* things happen, some people *watch* things happen and some people wonder, *hey, what happened?* If you watch and wonder, odds are you'll live an unfulfilled life, mired in the *ordinary zone*. If you believe the dream and you feel the dream, action must follow to *live* the dream. We must be crystal clear that *action* is the step which separates the dream from the delusion.

You believe you can have that Lamborghini, you can feel it, and you're ready to *take action* to acquire it. You start determining how hard you'll have to work to pull the finances together. You devise a savings plan so you won't have to break the bank and sacrifice other things which may be much more important than a material possession. Then you implement your plan. It may take a month, a year, a decade, who knows? It's your dream, your plan and you're taking decisive action—*and it's all on you.* If you do things just the right way and everything falls into place, lo and behold, one day that Lamborghini may be purring in your driveway at your disposal.

The three parts of dreaming we've outlined—*belief, feel* and *action*—are actually the process of *realistic visualization.* For instance, you're sitting in your favorite chair, pondering the possibilities of your life. As you become more and more relaxed you can actually feel yourself in a future scenario that doesn't seem foreign to you. You are perfectly comfortable and you are where you truly belong. It's picture perfect. It becomes so believable it's scary—*but it's also exciting!* You can reach out and touch the dream—*you can feel it.* The feeling is so real that it becomes an actual experience. Then, suddenly, an epiphany jolts you out of your dream and drives you to take action immediately. You know if you seize the moment your dream will certainly become reality.

With total confidence you start to act as if the dream is true. You walk the walk and talk the talk of a person ready for great things to happen. But, guess what—*the dream is true!* The dream *is* reality because you are engaged in the activity through which it will come into manifestation. What you're doing is spiritual and extraordinary. You're operating on faith which is the launching pad for all great things to happen. The real deal is that you're actually creating your own self-fulfilling prophecy through realistic visualization.

Now we know what a dream is. A dream is something you believe, feel and take action on, all sparked by realistic visualization. For clarity, there is one word which sums up the phenomenon of dreaming—*prolepsis*. Prolepsis is *the treating of a future event as if it had already happened.* For instance, you dream of going to college, then medical school and then becoming a practicing physician. Proleptically, in your mind, it is fact—*you are a physician.* It's already happened, it's just in the future. Sure, it may sound a little crazy, but prolepsis goes way beyond anticipation. In essence you are claiming your reality by *stepping* into your dream; and by doing so you become part of a time vortex which is your self-fulfilling prophecy. Taking that mental step is actually a quantum leap into your future. But, watch out, because when you do so, from that point forward, you can't hold anything back. You've gotta go for it!

What dreams have you believed, maybe even felt, but which you have not taken action on? It's a powerful question, maybe even a little scary, and only you can answer it. Now is the time to bring your dreams into reality. Take action! To the contrary, if you are not taking action on your dream, by default you will become part of someone else's dream. Is that in your best interest? Odds are it ain't, unless you're blessed and that person really, truly cares about your well-being. That being the case, whatever is holding you back, there are three little words just for you: *get over it.* Get over it right now, this instant. No excuses.

Following are a couple of ideas to help you take action on your dreams so you don't miss out on all the fun. First, always keep a pen and piece of paper on you or near you; or better yet, a mini tape recorder. Any time you have an idea that can bring you closer to realizing your dream, immediately capture it on paper or tape. For any dream you've had there may have been many ideas to make it come into reality. Some ideas are great, some are silly, some slip through the cracks; but, when you have them documented, you can reflect back on them when and if needed. Think of all ideas as lottery tickets. You don't want to make the mistake of throwing away a winner.

Second, over time a particular idea which may be horrible can transform into an unbelievable idea through brainstorming. There have been many times when I've talked an idea over with a friend or business associate that looked at it from a completely different angle. The challenge that most of us have is that we can only see things from one perspective, maybe two if you're extremely gifted. But a different person can see the same idea in a completely new light and suddenly the idea becomes brilliant.

To take it to a higher level, develop a group of trustworthy confidants with whom you share your ideas. They should form a tightly-knit coterie which has your best interest at heart. Napoleon Hill refers to it as a mastermind group in the classic *Think & Grow Rich*. Kicking around ideas in a group setting or brainstorming is an extremely healthy process. It can produce infinite options and miraculous results. After doing so don't be surprised if you don't recognize the original idea you brought to the table. Your dream may go through several transmutations before it's ready to be acted upon; or it may be totally canned and replaced by a new and improved idea. There's nothing wrong with that, just take it and run with it.

Lastly, there were many times I've had great ideas in the middle of the night and I couldn't sleep. I just kept tossing and turning in bed, spinning those ideas in my mind. But, you know what happened—*by the morning I talked myself out of the ideas.* I assassinated my own dreams by allowing doubt and lack of confidence to creep into my mind. Keep in mind a lot of those ideas that hit you in the middle of the night can be your most prolific ideas. They hit you in a super-conscious state while you're relaxed and your mind is open. Whatever you do, don't shortchange them. Get a grip on them and revisit them at a later point when you're a little more lucid. Many of those early morning ideas will bear fruit if you water them properly.

One final question to spin through your mind: *What dream do you believe and feel, that you will immediately take action on, which will allow you to influence your Dynamic Destiny and Live in the Power Zone?*

# DESIRE

*What do you desire to do or become more than anything else in the world and where has that desire taken you to this point in your life?*

*How you handle your desires can make or break you, so you must be very careful with them. What you say you desire says one thing, but the way you're conducting your life says it all.*

*S*itting in my favorite thinking chair one Sunday afternoon I began to think about how much I desired to be a published author and personal development coach. The catalyst was due to my corporate experience back in the mid-80's. I worked as a computer analyst which was a great job coming out of college. However, during that time I felt I had little influence over my life. I was told when to come in, when to go home, when to eat and when I could take a vacation. I could however go to the restroom whenever nature called, but that wasn't a great consolation prize. To make matters worse I was tormented by a drive to work in the most horrific rush hour traffic imaginable. Then I had to turn around and deal with the return trip home which was even more agonizing. It was pure hell.

What was most disconcerting was that I was told which career path to take. I knew exactly which way I wanted to go and what I wanted to be when I grew up, but the powers that be smacked me down. As time marched on I felt helpless and hopeless in corporate life. I couldn't *make anything happen,* which for me ain't the way to live life. In no way was my career leading me to my Dynamic Destiny, although at that time I had not even conceived the principle. Eventually I became so disgusted with myself that I decided to stop crying and do something about it.

In my car on the way to work I would listen to *The New Lead the Field* motivational tape by Earl Nightingale. I had been listening to it, off and on, prior to getting my cushy corporate position; but, during that arduous ride listening to it everyday started taking me to a higher mental level. On the way home I listened to vocabulary building tapes. I figured my ability to communicate would take me further than any other skill. Over the course of time I've found that to be very true. After listening to those tapes for about six months I finally got up enough nerve to start living my dream. I walked into the office one day said *I quit*. I left Corporate America and started my own business back in December of 1988.

What really happened is that I re-brainwashed myself for courage and success. The reason I say *re-brainwashed* is because we're all brainwashed to believe something. The issue is whether we realize what's happening, when it's happening and how it's happening. By definition brainwashing is *a forcible indoctrination to induce someone to give up basic political, social, or religious beliefs and attitudes and to accept contrasting regimented ideas.* As it relates to your Dynamic Destiny, it can be a scary proposition because some nasty stuff may be deeply rooted in your mind by outside forces. Mental trash is implanted through television, radio, music, commercials, propaganda, drugs, torture, repetition, confusion, psychological stress and probably a million other methods. However, for our purposes, we're mainly concerned about the phenomenon of self-induced brainwashing so you may *live in the power zone.*

Brainwashing goes on all day long in the foreground and background of your mind. Most background brainwashing can't be controlled because we're all subject to changing environments. As a warning, the majority of background brainwashing will keep you in ignorance and submerge you in self-limiting beliefs. That being said, always be cognizant of where you are, who you are with and what's going on. Whatever you do, keep your guard up and don't let your environment and outside forces eat you alive. On the other hand, to your great advantage, you have the power of choice to determine the type and intensity of the brainwashing in the foreground. If it is powerful enough it will build a shield of armor around your mind so most of the background brainwashing won't be able to penetrate and break down your psyche.

The way to mentally arm yourself is by only allowing particular concepts or ideologies to seep into your mind through your five senses. My primary re-brainwashing method was listening to tapes and CDs in my car. For long stretches of time I refused to listen to music and talk shows as I drove. I would only plug in motivational and educational tapes which opened the faucet for positive information to flow. Before you know it I was thinking at a much higher level. I started to believe things about myself which the average person might find unfathomable, yet the extraordinary person would deem exciting. Due to my experience I've concluded it's impossible to feed your mind with too much powerful and enlightening information. We all need a little more to keep the fire burning. Much to my delight, one of the by-products of my re-brainwashing process is *The Dynamic Destiny Principle.*

What has brought us together so we may exchange ideas is a defining moment in my life. That defining moment was neither a positive or negative experience, it was simply a decision at a fork in the road. Unknowingly the direction I chose made it crystal clear who I am and what I'm about, although I didn't know it at the time. As a result I'm able to share with you my philosophy on what it takes to become the person you've always dreamed of.

When I was in the fourth grade I took a musical aptitude test. Since I did well I was given the opportunity to choose the instrument I wanted to study; and I chose the trumpet. To tell you the truth, I really wanted to play the trombone. It was bigger, you could slide the horn in and out and it looked like it was fun to play. Mistakenly I said I wanted to play the trumpet, thinking it was a trombone. When the music teacher handed me the trumpet I looked at it sort of puzzled, but I didn't fight it. I quietly took it, began lessons and started practicing. It was obvious that I had some talent and by far I was the best trumpeter in the grade school. Then I went on to junior high and high school and I still stood out among the trumpeters.

During high school I was turned on to jazz. I remember buying Louis Armstrong and Dizzy Gillespie albums and listening to them incessantly. My Aunt Pepsi gave me my first Miles Davis album—*Miles Davis Greatest Hits*—and I became a jazz fiend. I would visualize myself jamming with Dizzy and Miles and electrifying the crowd. I dreamed of going on European tours and performing to standing room only crowds with my idols. My desire for the trumpet and jazz music was growing by leaps and bounds, so much so that I applied to the esteemed Berklee College of Music in Boston.

Berklee was definitely one of the top tier schools in the country and I vividly remember visiting the campus to determine if I should enroll. It was so exciting being around other musicians; however, to this day I don't know exactly what stopped me from attending Berklee. My best guess is that it was some form of subconscious fear. I know I was scared to leave home, but I know I also had a fear of failure pumping through my veins. Regrettably my desire to attend Berklee didn't override those fears. Instead I opted to stay home and attend Rutgers University in Piscataway, New Jersey. In hindsight that turned out to be the best thing for me.

During the early eighties the atmosphere at Rutgers was perfect for an up and coming jazz musician. There was an esteemed trumpet instructor there, as well as a respected jazz ensemble leader. Rutgers was the incubator for many talented and successful young musicians who subsequently went on to live their dreams; however, there was one student I met my first day at jazz ensemble rehearsal who had the greatest impact on me, trumpeter Terence Blanchard. Terence has since gone on to tour the world, produce many great albums and even write many great movie scores. He's now regarded as one of the great jazz musicians on the scene today and he's definitely my favorite trumpeter.

Before going to Rutgers I was a big fish in a little pond coming from Linden, New Jersey. Actually, Linden was more like a little puddle drying up on a hot summer day with respect to jazz music. During our first jazz ensemble rehearsal at Rutgers the musical director, Paul Jeffrey, wanted to hear everyone play individually, so I gave it my best shot. Actually I thought I did quite well and I had my chest out for a moment. Then Terence played. To this day I still can't believe how awesome he was at 19 years of age. It was by far the best trumpet playing I had ever heard up to that point in my life. You could sense his desire to be a stellar trumpet player. Of course, I was totally embarrassed because I thought I played something hip and cool. My ego took a huge blow that day. It was totally deflated and I never recovered from it. I was just making noise compared to the mellifluous melodies flowing from Terence's horn. At my absolute best I could play five percent of what he could play. It was a very humbling experience.

That evening I made a critical decision which set the sail for the rest of my life. I decided to major in computer science, while at the same time pursue a musical career. At that time of my life, without realizing it, it was the biggest decision I'd ever made. Computers were fun and I had an inclination toward them in high school. I was a pretty decent math student and I was able to think logically, so why not go for it and get the computer science degree? That decision provided safety and security because I figured I'd always be able to get a job working with computers; but, that same decision would also cramp my musical development. The music students who truly desired to succeed devoted their lives to their craft. They gave it all they had while comparatively I was just devoting a little spare time to the cause.

The final nail in the coffin of my musical career came when I went to visit Terence in New York while he was living with another fine musician, alto sax player Donald Harrison. Donald actually picked up my trumpet and played it far better than I ever have to this day. I was embarrassed and devastated. The thought of a saxophone player outplaying me, with my own horn, was a hit below the belt. The pain was too much to bear and I totally wimped out. My musical aspirations went up in smoke.

When I look back upon that time I've come to the conclusion that I really didn't *desire* to be a musician. I was full of fear and unable to shake it. I was fearful of not making it big. I was fearful of being a great musician and never getting recognition during my lifetime. I was fearful of being flat broke and pitiful. I was fearful that I really didn't have what it would take to get up on stage and please my audience. I was just scared stiff. I was determined not to face those fears by majoring in computer science.

That whole experience has brought me to some heart-felt conclusions regarding desire. Desiring is not saying what you want, nor is it longing or wishing for something which you do not possess. Regarding my so-called musical ambitions, I wasn't aware of it at the time, but I was longing and wishing. The real deal is that I was taking decisive action on my computer science degree, which thankfully I obtained four years later. Forget about what comes out of your mouth because talk is dirt cheap. Anything can be said, but only a few can back up the talk. Terence never told me what he desired—*he was just making it happen.* He desired world tours, CD's and movie scores, and he got what he deserved through hard work. He wasn't blowing hot air; instead he just blew into his horn and produced at a high level. Thanks to Terence I learned what true desire is more than twenty years ago. In a weird way he is living my dream and I admire him for having the courage to pull it off. So, as Tupac would say, *"I ain't mad at 'cha...got nuthin' but luv for ya...do ya thing."*

Let's take a look at Joe who works hard on his job. He's on his way home thinking about how great it would be to write that book he's been putting off for years. He desired to be an author way back when, but things just kept getting between him and what he said he wanted. Joe gets home, puts the key in the door, comes in and kisses his wife hello. He's bombarded by the kids who demand his attention for help with homework or whatever other mischief they have in mind. After they have a great dinner Joe decides to relax, have a beer and watch a little television. It's been a long day and he finally gets a moment to decompress. Then after a couple of hours he retires to bed. The next morning the routine starts all over again.

Then, thank God it's finally Friday so Joe can really stretch out and relax over the weekend. Maybe he'll play with the kids, visit a few friends and do a couple of mindless chores around the house. Soon vacation time rolls around. Joe books a road trip so he and his wife can break the monotony. He feels you have to get away sometimes and recharge the batteries, otherwise you'll go crazy. After he's recharged he'll come back stronger than ever so he can jump back in the rat race and start the cycle all over again.

Many of us are familiar with that scenario. A nice guy gets a cushy job, is a great husband and father, and does what he's expected to do. He and his family are secure and everyone is happy. As time marches on Joe's desire to write that book takes a back seat to his other responsibilities and he never commits pen to paper. What we must recognize is writing that book is not a *true desire*. Joe's real desire in life is to do whatever it is that he is currently doing, not what he says he wants to do. He wants to be a great husband and father, and he is. He wants to progress at his job, and he does. Nonetheless, if he really desired to write that book, he would write that book, period. Joe would not let anything stand in his way. But, over the course of time, it became really comfortable to hide behind his other responsibilities and not get the job done.

Question: Is it possible to be a great husband and father, advance professionally, and in the midst of all that action, write a book or satisfy some other desire? Of course it is. It's not a super-human feat. Providing for his wife and kids is the most important aspect of Joe's life and that's the way it should be. We would all agree that he can't be selfish in satisfying his desires and leave everyone else in the dust. Many people have dealt with Joe's familial responsibilities—*and even more*—and managed to realize their desires and *live in the power zone.*

Since you're investing valuable time in this book, which you will never recover, your desire for something special must be great. There's absolutely no doubt there is something spectacular within you, kicking and screaming to be unleashed. Now that you're totally aware of its existence, if you continue to suppress it, there will be nothing but anguish in your future. *It's time to quench your thirst.* All you must do is *find* or *create* the time to liberate what desire is inside and the complexion of your life will improve dramatically. You have 24-7 just like everyone else, it's simply a matter of how you carve up your day and invest your time. When you have true desire you'll make sure there's always a slice of time dedicated to it. If you find you can't do that, it's time to make some serious changes and get a life.

If every day you sit in front of your TV and watch soap operas all day long, your desire is to be a professional soap opera watcher. Unfortunately that job doesn't pay too well, but at least you're accomplishing a goal. It may be a shock to you, but there are plenty of people in that profession. It's an easy job to get, you don't have to work that hard and there's no advanced degree required. From what I hear it's quite popular and it's a heckuva lot of fun. But, will it produce the lifestyle you desire?

What do you think would happen if you worked every day for an hour to get into tip-top physical condition? You wake up craving to hit the gym, break a serious sweat and burn some calories. Obviously that's your desire and you'll probably be in tip-top physical condition because of it. And just because you're doing something worthwhile, serendipitously your desire may lead you into personal training or some other health related profession where you could earn a living—*and have the time of your life*. There's nothing like getting paid to do what you love!

Looking again at my situation, I never really desired to be a jazz musician because I wasn't willing to take action. Clearly I desire to be an inspiring speaker, writer and personal trainer because I'm *doing* those things. I speak, write and train clients all the time— *I live it, I breathe it*. Those are my passions and I *find* and *create* time for them. It took some time, but I got over the fact that I missed the jazz ship years ago. Then I promised myself that the next ship that came to port I would not miss for anything in the world. Consequently, you're now taking pleasure in reading my second book and my third is waiting in the wings to be thrust into action.

If you feel you've missed a ship or two, don't fret. Step back, take a few power breaths, shake the dust from your eyes and take a look at your life. Actually you may have to step way, way back and get totally away from your surroundings. Get away from everyone you know, everything you're familiar with and move out of your comfort zone. The reason to do so is to induce mental clarity. Oftentimes we're too entrenched in our own muck and mire to see ourselves clearly. If you shake things up a bit, I'd bet my last nickel you would be able to see that there's another ship for you to catch. It may be far off in the horizon, but it's approaching quickly.

Right now you're on my ship, sailing on these printed words, and we're having a grand time; but, you can't hang out with me forever. Be mindful your ship will be docked before you know it. It's imperative that you're ready to seize the moment because the window of opportunity will open and shut in the blinking of an eye; and if you hesitate you can best believe it will sail off into the sunset without you. There are plenty of other hungry individuals who will jump on your ship and claim it for themselves. And don't be chagrined when someone else is waving goodbye to you, smiling and thanking you for missing the opportunity. The fact is opportunity does not linger and it waits for no one.

Opportunity can also be cruel. Even if you jump on your ship and you're now at the helm, you can always be replaced. Don't be arrogant and think someone can't take your job. Squeezing through the door is cool, but just gettin' in ain't good enough. You've gotta get the job done. If you can't handle the pressure you will get the boot. You must continually rise to the occasion and perform at the highest level, through diligent preparation and deft execution. It must be clear that opportunity doesn't need you, you need it.

Another question: *What in the world are you doing with your time that could cause you to miss your ship?* What desires are you acting on, consciously or subconsciously, which could divert your attention? Think deeply because the answer will set the sail for the rest of your life. When you think about it, it's really simple. What you acted on in the past *was* your desire; what you're acting on right now, today, *is* your desire; and what you will act on in the future *will be* your desire. If you look around you the satisfaction of your desires would be your surroundings. You are thick in the middle of all that you desire, based on everything that you have acted on and everything that you have not acted on. Simply put, *you are what you do and you do what you are.* That being said, the only thing that could cause you to miss that ship would be the type of person you are. Some people miss ships and some people don't. On the extreme side some people are chronic ship-missers who seem to fumble away every opportunity.

Years ago I had a friend, Andrew, who was such a character. He was set up with an incredible opportunity by another friend, Tommy, to perform with a jazz band. The band had a two month European tour scheduled and all it needed to be in peak form was a piano player. Andrew fit the bill. He was extremely talented and came highly recommended by Tommy. The beauty of the gig was that all expenses were taken care of. Andrew didn't have to take a dime out of his pocket—*not that he had one anyway.* All he had to do was play the piano, have a good time and get paid doing what he loved to do. Up until that time Andrew was having extreme difficultly getting steady gigs, but it seemed as though finally all the stars were lining up in his favor.

Everything was systems go with the band taking off in a few days. Of course, you know what happened—*Andrew missed the bon voyage flight to Paris.* It was the opportunity of a lifetime, but Andrew was simply the type of person who kept on shooting himself in the foot. No one knows what caused him to miss that flight and no one cared. He simply wasn't dependable. After that debacle Andrew found it difficult to get other gigs of that stature. Being labeled a chronic ship-misser certainly didn't help.  Needless to say the band picked up another piano player once it crossed the Atlantic and the tour was a raving success.

Whatever you do, don't follow Andrew's lead.  Be the type of person who is known for taking advantage of what is laid before you.  Above all else, be dependable.  People want to know they can count on you when it counts; hence, dependability is far more important than ability.  You can be the best in the world at what you do, but if you let people down they'll never forget it.  Most of all you don't want to let yourself down.  It should be obvious that if you can't be counted on at crunch time, your desire is questionable at best.

As you set sail your most important challenge will be to wage war against two insidiously powerful foes.  They are silent killers and have blocked the path of many seeking to reach their ports of call.  They're always lurking and always looking for an opportunity to wedge in between you and your desires.  You can't see 'em, you can't touch 'em, but you will feel their devastating impact.  Under no circumstances are they to be underestimated; however, with great desire you can beat 'em every time.  Beware of *procrastination* and *self-imposed limitations*.

In the past it wasn't any person or any particular thing that stopped me from being successful—*it was all on me.* I was dreadfully wrong when I thought it was another person or thing that stood between me and what I desired. That was simply my excuse for not getting the job done. I was constantly beat down by procrastination and self-imposed limitations mainly because I was unaware of how deceptive they are. They sneak into your life when you least expect it, so you always have to keep your guard up. Then one day I got real lucky. I was listening to a recording by my favorite speaker and business philosopher, Jim Rohn, and he made it crystal clear who the true enemies were and where they resided—*in my head.* At that point I became empowered because I realized I could overcome them, if I chose to.

What's so funny is that most of us start off every working day procrastinating by hitting the snooze button on our alarm clocks. I hit mine at least thrice every morning. The great writer Henry Miller believed, *"Life, as it is called, is for most of us one long postponement."* Maybe Mr. Miller would have agreed that the cure for procrastination is simply *do it now.* Whatever it is that you want to do or need to do to satisfy your desire, *do it now.* Don't think about it;

don't talk about it; stop playing around with it; and just *do it now*. Beyond that, continually visualize how devastating your future could be if you did not take on the task you've been putting off. If that visualization ain't enough to get you motivated, you must do some soul searching regarding your desire. Maybe you don't want it bad enough. If that's true, it's time to move on to something else. But if you do want it bad enough, step up to the plate and *do it now*.

To combat self-imposed limitations a friend told me something years ago that I'll never forget. He said, *"Never sell yourself short. Never, ever sell yourself short. You're a unique child of the universe with unlimited potential."* You've gotta know that's true. Impose no limitations upon yourself. Even more important, never let anyone else's limitations define you. There are some people who may delight in destroying your spirit, but you've gotta believe in what the universe has bestowed upon you. You must also know that you deserve success. If you continue to work hard; treat others with dignity and respect; remain sincere; and be willing to help others succeed, you deserve to be rewarded and you deserve to realize your desires.

Defeating procrastination and self-imposed limitations will allow everything to fall in place. The days of missing ships and watching opportunities slip through your fingers like grains of sand are over. It's a new day and all that you desire is there for the taking. Ponder this: *What desire will you fuel to take you to the pinnacle of your success and manifest your Dynamic Destiny?*

# DECISIONS

*What decision have you made, or not made, that has put you in the position you're in?*

*You can't sit at the fork in the road forever when it comes time to make a decision. You must commit.*

*M*aking decisions can be confusing and scary. You're sitting at a fork in the road, with everything on the line, and whaddaya do? There were times I was terrified to step one way or the other for fear of losing money, time and once my life. The thought of making an error in judgment in those sticky situations took my heart more times than I'd like to admit. Even during those times when making the wrong decision wouldn't hurt me that much, I was still scared to decide. There always seemed to be one more mental roadblock that overpowered my decision making process.

One big hurdle with decision-making is that it requires you to think. Sadly that's asking way too much of some of us. Mental laziness oftentimes kicks in as many would prefer to sit back with a bag of popcorn and watch *As the World Turns*. On the other hand, there's an even bigger hurdle with decision-making: it forces you to commit. Commitment is a serious proposition because it binds you to a particular course of action. No one wants to feel *stuck* because of a decision, so the tendency is to avoid commitment at all costs. But, make no mistake about it, the fear of committing and being stuck can be fatalistic to your Dynamic

Destiny. We all want a little wiggle room to get out of a sticky situation, but you've got to be brave enough to make a decision and stick with it. It's the only way to thrive and *live in the power zone.*

In 1993 there was a movie entitled *Point of No Return* starring Bridgette Fonda as Nina. Nina was a convicted murderess and drug abuser who was sentenced to be executed. After her *faked* execution and funeral she was given the option to become a sophisticated government assassin or deal with the prospect of a *real* execution. Grasping for life, Nina took the assassin option; but committing to it meant she could never go back to a normal life. She found out the hard way that if she attempted to retire prematurely, she would be assassinated by the same government she worked for. Clearly Nina was beyond a point of no return as a direct result of her commitment. Of course, very few decisions are that grave where your physical life is in jeopardy, but the *quality* of your life is at risk all the time.

To overcome the fear of making the wrong decision the first step is to determine the long-range consequences. In other words, *how much and for how long will you be burned if you take the wrong path?* If you won't get burned at all, don't sweat it.

For instance, where should you go for dinner tonight? If you make a bad choice you've only wasted one evening, a couple of hours and a few bucks. Surprisingly some people agonize over such a simple decision. It ain't worth it.

What about the decision to start a business? That decision can have long-reaching ramifications—*and you can be scorched severely if you make a mistake.* Some things to consider are where will you get the start-up money from? Who will you market to? How long will it take to turn a profit? What's the probability of going belly up? When those questions echo through your mind it becomes real tough to pull the trigger and go for it. It's clear to see the rewards of jumping into entrepreneurship, which include financial freedom and security, being your own boss, taking control of your life, etcetera. On the other hand you can also vividly imagine the pain you could cause for yourself and your family if everything goes haywire. For that type of decision you must be disciplined and mentally tough to weigh every option. Far too many people foolishly jump in the water without really thinking it through—*as I have more than once.*

After weighing the long-range consequences of the decision, how do you decide? As simple as it seems, my favorite decision-making technique is the coin flip. There's a lot more that you can do with a coin than start a football game. If you have two options and you're 50-50 regarding which way to go, the coin flip is the perfect solution. Just pull out your Susan B. Anthony dollar coin, toss it in the air and let Susie do all the heavy lifting. If heads comes up you simply take option A; if it's tails, option B. But what if heads comes up and you decide you don't want option A?

What actually happens is the coin flip method doesn't make the decision, it simply pushes you in one direction or another. By forcing your hand it often reveals which way you're leaning because you never really feel 50-50 between two distinct options. Additionally, when you're pushed in a particular direction, other factors may be uncovered for your consideration. It sounds simple, but it works.

How about when you have multiple options and a coin flip won't do the job? My favorite method is to take each option and give it a rating, based on certain criteria. Let's say you're in the market to purchase a car. Faced with three or more prospects your criteria for rating may include horsepower, comfort, stereo system, navigation system, gas mileage, heating, air conditioning and/or maintenance costs. Rate each car based on your criteria on a scale of from 1 to 10. Total up your points and the car with the most points wins. It's a done deal.

What if it's a *go* or *no go* decision? Should you decide to move forward or just wait a little while longer until you're absolutely, positively, undeniably sure? For instance, you're looking to purchase a home and you find a swanky condo that overlooks Central Park in Manhattan. It's exactly what you've been searching for and it perfectly fits your image. You're comfortable where you currently live and you're under no pressure to move out, but this is the opportunity of a lifetime. It's expensive, but not out of your reach. All you have to do is juggle a few things around and everything will gently fall into place. You're ecstatic that your offer to purchase is accepted and you start planning your first soiree. When you get back to your apartment you start doing some serious number crunching to make it all happen, but something doesn't feel right. For some reason the financial burden seems to be a little more than you imagined. You become indecisive and start to doubt whether you should move forward with the purchase at all.

The beauty of the *go* or *no go* decision is there's usually no major downside if you decide not to go for it. If you don't consummate the deal on the condo you don't really lose anything, just a little bit of time. You may be a little peeved with yourself for not being brave enough to pull the trigger, but you'll get over it. On the other hand, if you do go for it all hell might break loose. You could lose your cushy job and slip into foreclosure. With *go* or *no go* decisions it's best to be completely comfortable with moving forward. Weigh the risks and go for it, but only if you can mentally and/or financially absorb the shock of the downside being triggered. If you can't, back off and be patient until another opportunity comes your way.

What if you have one of my favorites, a *do nothing* decision? A decision needs to be made and you decide not to decide. The thing to consider is what would happen if you hung out in the bleachers and took no action? For example, once my wife and I were on the beautiful island of St. Thomas luxuriating on the beach. As the waiter delivered our third round of Piña Coladas my dear wife received a disturbing phone call from her secretary, Nancy. After 30 seconds she decided to hang up on Nancy which completely nonplused me. I asked her, *"Honey, are you insane?"* She replied, *"Yes, when I'm on vacation I am insane, especially after my third Piña Colada. The problem will take care of itself by tomorrow morning. Wait and see."* Of course, she was correct, as wives usually are. There was no way she was going to exhaust any mental energy while deepening her tan when the perfect solution was obvious. Nancy figured everything out on her own and everything was cool.

If you're confronted with a problem, make no decision about it and take no action, sometimes the problem goes away by itself. As you're working on your Dynamic Destiny you'll be bombarded with decisions—some critical, some not—and most likely you won't have the mental energy to attack all of them. You just have to sense which problems will resolve without your presence so you can spend your valuable time on the important decisions that truly need your input. Keep in mind most problems and decisions won't go away without you exerting some mental energy. Don't be lazy and be prepared to put on your thinking cap.

There are many decision-making techniques you can use, so I'll ask you to further investigate decision-making on your own precious time. But, for your purpose, which is the realization of your Dynamic Destiny, there is something much more important you must consider. There will come a point in time when you have a dream that you will take action on. Your desire will be so powerful that you devise a plan to bring the dream to life. You begin implementing the plan, with excitement and enthusiasm, and you feel unstoppable. Then comes a critical point when the initial excitement and enthusiasm start to wane. For some inexplicable reason you simply run out of steam. You were gung-ho and ready to take on the world in the beginning and then you ran smack dab into a brick wall. No one can tell you why, it just seems to work like that.

How many people do you think make New Year's Eve resolutions, but near the end of January the wheels come flying off and they cave in? Many people can't even make it to January 2$^{nd}$—*and that's a stretch*. I have a friend who swore to suck down his last cigarette on December 31$^{st}$. He was fired up and ready to jump on the highway to optimal health. His doctor said he had to make a change or else, so at 11:59 p.m. he took a few more glorious drags of his last cancer stick. It looked like it felt so good that I almost wished I was a smoker. He then flicked his cigarette away with indignation as we started counting down the last ten seconds of the year. Everyone could see how overjoyed he was to start off the New Year as a non-smoker. By 2:00 a.m. he was climbing the walls. By 3:00 a.m. he and another former smoker decided to fire 'em up. They ran smack-dab into a brick wall. They didn't have the heart to break through it and decided to have a smoke and not deal with it.

The point is you can only sail but so far on the winds of excitement and enthusiasm. To continue to move forward you must be committed and unwilling to turn back. When it starts to get tough and you're ready to bail out, that's when you must make the real decision: *Do I really want to go for it?* You're agonizing at the fork in the road and there's no turning back—*you've reached the point of no return.* To complicate matters there's no one who can help you make the decision to really go for it because only you know what you truly desire—*if not, go back to the previous chapter.* So, how do you turn your agony into ecstasy?

Simply put, the decision to really go for it is a piece of cake, if you truly desire to live your dreams. To realize your Dynamic Destiny and *live in the power zone* you don't have a choice—*you must go for it.* If you don't you'll be kicking yourself in the rear end for God knows how long. Your greatness lies way beyond the fork in the road and you will definitely navigate through many forks to realize it. Time marches on and so must you, just keep in mind the path toward your Dynamic Destiny will be riddled with trials and tribulations impossible to imagine at the time you make the decision. There are so many things you just can't see because there are so many things you just don't know. It can be due to a lack of experience, myopic vision or, as my great-grandmother would say, having a hard head and not listening.

Regarding what you don't know, it can plant fear in your mind about the consequences of your decision. That fear could throw you into a *realm of instability* where you become shell-shocked and unable to move forward. The number one key to influence your Dynamic Destiny is to confidently move forward using all of your talents, in a realm of instability, when you don't have all the answers and you have no clue what questions will be thrown at you. American writer Erica Jong believed, *"Everyone has a talent. What is rare is to follow the talent to the dark place where it leads."* To get through this lifetime, live a life of fulfillment and succeed at your highest level, deep faith must be invoked to *live in the power zone* and walk through that dark place. It's a decisive moment when you must be audacious because sometimes you gotta go when you just don't know.

For instance, I retired from Corporate America and started my first business at age 25. I had no experience and no practical knowledge regarding business except what I read in books. On the positive side I had hopes, dreams and enough money to last me for six months until my business started to take off. Beyond those six months I had no clue what was going to happen. I was in a total realm of instability and it was sink or swim. Being the maverick that I've been known to be, I went ahead and jumped in anyway. It wasn't the smartest thing to do, but sometimes smarts can get in the way of progress. To my advantage my commitment was rock solid and I decided to fight it out, until the final bell, and cut off all other possibilities of retreat. Fortunately things took off for me within that six month time period and I haven't looked back.

Again, your conviction and commitment must be rock solid. There will always be doubts and fears because you're human. Sure, life can be dangerous, but if you decide not to move forward because of doubts and fears, you probably shouldn't roll out of bed in the morning. You can't let those two emotions be an anchor around your neck when it's time to start sailing. If you are to fear anything, let it be the fear of not making a decision and living a life of regret, regardless of whether you made the right or wrong decision. You're human and some of your decisions will stink—*that's life.* Some decisions will bring you to your knees as tears flow from your eyes. Nevertheless, if you work through your fear, you'll also make some incredibly great decisions and have flashes of brilliance.

At this time there are three critical decisions I implore you to make. What you decide will determine exactly how high you will climb in this world and if you will *live in the power zone.* The first decision is a piece of cake. You must simply *decide to do what is legally correct.* Unfortunately some cross the line and find themselves trapped in a quagmire of illicit activity. The next thing you know the justice system puts them on a slow boat to the penitentiary. It ain't pretty and what I'm really saying is I refuse to visit you in jail any time soon, so you know what you have to do—*or better yet, not do.* And even if you don't get caught crossing the line and hurting others, you never really get off scot-free. What goes around comes around, so do the right thing.

The second decision is easy also, but it can be a little tricky. Assuming you stay on the right side of the law, you must now *decide to do what is morally correct.* Many people feel just because it's legal, it's fair game. I'm not too sure about that one. It seems like a morally bankrupt philosophy that at best will land you in spiritual purgatory. Morality is a sticky issue because everyone's sense of it is a little different. What one man would do another man would never consider. Accordingly, it's unrealistic to expect us to agree on every moral issue. In the continuing effort to police yourself, if the action you take doesn't hurt anyone, you'll probably have good karma and fare well. Additionally, if you strive for win-win scenarios, personally and professionally, even if you make errors in judgment, you'll probably be golden.

The third decision is the most important decision you'll ever make. It's actually an ongoing decision that will require keen introspection mixed with extraordinary discipline. You must simply *decide to do what is in your best interest.* I know, you think I'm joking, but I'm dead serious. It sounds so easy to do, but as the American songwriters George and Ira Gershwin may have agreed, *It Ain't Necessarily So.*

Many people are rowing across a pond, while punching holes in their own boat—*and they wonder why they're sinking!* For some bizarre reason they're engaging in self-sabotage, doing things and thinking thoughts they know will cause eventual implosion. And, by the way, we're all subject to self-sabotage, due mainly to lack of focus and lack of discipline. Some of us struggle with it every single day. Without proper focus and discipline, you can seamlessly segue out of harmony into cacophony as discord slowly takes control of your life. During that insidious process you can decide to do some really stupid things that are definitely not in your best interest. There ain't no gentle way to spin it, some things are just plain stupid.

For instance, for the past 20-plus years I've been engaged in what's known as a *vegan* lifestyle. It means that I've taken animal products out of my diet—no beef, no pork, no chicken, no fish. In addition, I avoid animal derivatives such as milk, eggs, butter and cheese. And when we finally get together for dinner you wouldn't see me eat any cake, ice-cream or candy, unless it's made in a special way. To many it seems extremely ascetic, but for me it's a lot of fun. It's amazing what you can do with fruits and veggies. However, there are times when I break down and eat potato chips and other junk food. It doesn't violate anything previously mentioned, but it's still junk; and as a gentleman once asked me, *"Why would you put junk in your body?"*

Well, for me, eating junk food is stupid. I know better than that, but I consciously succumb to self-sabotage by putting junk in my body. If I didn't know any better it would be a totally different story, but I do. It's purely lack of focus and lack of discipline. Many people would feel it's harmless; a little bit won't hurt; you can get away with that; everything in moderation is cool, etcetera. To me none of that matters because *I know* it is self-sabotage. My body expects more from me. Nevertheless, if someone else decides to eat junk food, beef, fried chicken, any form of swine or anything else I don't eat, I don't have a problem with it—*more power to you.* You've got to live your life. You can sit right next to me, do your thing and eat like it's your last supper; and as you gormandize, I'll pat you on the back and watch you enjoy yourself. For better or for worse, it's your decision. However, if you *know* what you're eating is not in your best interest, you've got to reconsider what you're doing.

And, for the record, please don't buy into the *everything in moderation* philosophy. It is completely bogus and deciding to adopt it can be extremely hazardous. Many things shouldn't be done moderately, if at all. You've got to keep it real and recognize what you should and shouldn't be doing for *your best interest.* You're not perfect, so there will be times where you will work against yourself, but don't rationalize and say something is cool when it obviously ain't.

For example, you're on a diet and doing quite well with it. You know what you're not supposed to eat and you've been extremely disciplined; as a result, the pounds are flyin' off—*and you're getting hotter by the day.* You're hangin' out one evening showin' off your new and improved body and your best friend forever says, *"Try this, it's so good. Just a little bit won't hurt. C'mon, the best way to live is everything in moderation. You can't be too serious, you won't have any fun!"* You fall for the sales pitch and dig in. The next thing you know you've fallen off the bandwagon and you're wallowing in the dirt. Everyday you're *moderately* shoving things in your mouth that *moderately* pack the pounds back on. So much for that diet.

What would you think if a member of Alcoholics Anonymous adopted the *everything in moderation* philosophy? You have a buddy you're proud of who kicked alcoholism in the gluteus maximus. He's been clean and sober for years and is a great inspiration at his AA meetings. But, for some quirky reason, he does an about face and decides to have *only* one glass of wine per week. That's fairly moderate, isn't it? It couldn't be that bad for him, could it? Of course, that decision could be the beginning of the end. One sip could open the floodgates a little too much and we soon have a state of emergency. For your buddy one drink is too many and a million is not enough. His only chance for survival is total elimination of alcohol from his program—*moderation ain't happenin'.*

Let's take a peek at a few popular self-sabotage decisions in action. For instance, is it in your best interest to *decide* not to get proper exercise? Is it in your best interest to *decide* to smoke cigarettes? Is it in your best interest to *decide* to not save or invest money for your future? Is it in your best interest to *decide* to procrastinate? Is it in your best interest to *decide* to work in a profession that is unfulfilling? Last, but not least, is it in your best interest to *decide* to be miserable? Believe it or not, those are all decisions. We could kick around questions like that all day long and the answers are blindingly obvious. We both know the deal. Since those questions are so easy, let's take a look at a tough one: *Is it in your best interest to decide to not give 100% in pursuit of your dreams and aspirations?* We both know the answer to that one too—*of course not!* It's foolish, if not downright dangerous, to decide to give anything less than 100%. Regardless of the obvious, why have so many people decided to give a halfhearted effort?

Imagine you're the star running back on a football team. The ball is snapped and the quarterback hands it off to you. Within a split second you see a 265-pound linebacker quickly approaching whose job is simple: hit you hard, slam you to the ground and make it as painful as possible. He just signed a lucrative contract to make you hurt and he gets a bonus if he makes you quit. Simply put, he's extremely motivated. You can best believe if you give anything less than 100% when you collide with him your health will be in serious jeopardy. The linebacker is definitely giving 100%, if not more, so you have no choice but to match his intensity. Likewise, you must decide to meet your dreams and aspirations with intensity. The obstacles you must bore through to attain them are fierce. If you're not man or woman enough to make that decision and do the right thing, you may as well sit at home and watch the game on TV.

Maybe you're not a football enthusiast and the business world is your gridiron. You're delighted because you've just been hired as Chief Executive Officer of Me, Inc. Since you're the top dog you must make the right decisions to ensure Me, Inc. is a profitable business enterprise. If you fail to do so, your employment contract will be terminated— *nuthin' personal, strictly business.* Well, here's the latest newsflash: *Whether you like it or not, you are the CEO of Me, Inc.* You're also the Founder, President and Chairman of the Board. You're the whole enchilada! It's all about you and you can best believe that your dreams and aspirations will certainly be terminated if you don't make the decision to give 100% or more. Surely you already know that, but it's best to keep it in the forefront of your mind. So what are you going to do about it?

In 2007, after suffering through the subprime debacle and subsequent economic recession, I made a gruesome, self-sabotage decision. I hit a series of financial road bumps and I desperately needed some cash yesterday. In a flash of insanity I decided to take a job doing telephone sales. And don't get me wrong, telephone sales is a tremendous opportunity, provided you're associated with the right company. In the beginning I was gung-ho about the job and ready to take on the world. I expected to make a decent dollar since the job was full commission. Of course, the company sold all sales agents on the possibility of making unlimited income. I wasn't dumb enough to fall for that old trick, but I figured *I gotta do what I gotta do.* I had to eat and I didn't want my wife to divorce me and take half of nuthin'.

After the first month I knew I'd made a colossal mistake—*and, of course, my better half told me I was stepping into dog manure from the very beginning.* The job was a boiler room which lacked all semblances of professional decorum; and that ain't my style. When you've always strived to conduct yourself with grace and dignity, it's tough to do it any other way. Every night I came home hating myself, feeling like a stupid idiot, because I knew I was committing the worst of sins—*wasting time.* My spirit was tanking quickly, I lost my mojo and I was in a danger zone nightmare. For those reasons and others I decided I had to sprint outta there as quickly as possible.

One evening I came home totally drained after another horrific 10 hours at that gig and I had a powwow with my wife. I told her, *"I gotta get outta there before I kill myself."* We both agreed that wasn't in the best interest of my Dynamic Destiny, so she supported my decision to leave. The next day she came in from her business all beat up and said her secretary quit. She was perplexed about finding a replacement and she asked for my opinion. At that point the obvious smacked some sense into me and I decided, *"Honey, I'll work for you!"* Obviously she loved that option because then she could boss me around at home and at work. What a life!

What really happened was that I woke up and realized that I'm the CEO of Me, Inc. and I was in a funk, underperforming and doing an atrocious job. As a result my dreams and aspirations were in serious jeopardy. The only solution was to step up my game and get Me, Inc. back on track. Hence, as the CEO of Me, Inc., I decided that I was way too good for that job. I had too much talent and ambition to throw in the trash. Once that decision was made I stopped self-sabotaging and everything started to turn around. Good things began to happen and I got my mojo back. The moral of the story: *Whatever you do, don't forget who you work for. It's purely your decision!*

Life is just one fork in the road after another. Decisions, decisions, decisions—they will determine your future. Something to think about: *What decision and commitment are you going to make right now, this instant, to live your life and influence your Dynamic Destiny?*

# DEVOTION

*What worthy cause are you devoted to and how has it affected your life?*

*Devotions are tricky because you can put so much of yourself on the line. Be careful how much you sacrifice.*

*W*hen someone mentions the word *devotion* I think back to the countless times I fell hopelessly in love. I remember being so badly smitten I would do anything to be with the lady of the moment; yet, strange things always seemed to happen with those relationships. Most of them soured way too quickly for my palate. One minute I was savoring a fine glass of cabernet sauvignon and all of a sudden I was sipping balsamic vinegar with a broken heart.

Once I was rejected in the first grade by the prettiest girl in the school. Many relationships later I was seeing a beautiful young lady who told me, as she was breaking up with me, she didn't owe me an explanation. She was so cold about it. Her words were like a dagger plunging deeper into my heart. In my mind all I could hear was the soul songstress Roberta Flack singing *Killing Me Softly;* although, as I look back, I had some serious issues. I was asking to be rejected and mercilessly kicked to the curb because of my delusions about the relationships I was in. At that time I didn't understand what devotion was really all about.

Devotion is the most perplexing of the Dynamic Destiny concepts because you must be extremely careful regarding what you're devoted to. When you put your heart and soul on the line for someone or something that doesn't deserve it, it can be a huge blow to your spirit, not to mention the pain and humiliation you may have to endure.

Devotion is also precarious because you have to sacrifice. Far too often we sacrifice way too much and gain way too little. Yes, it's noble to give, but it's important to know how much you can give without tearing yourself apart in the process. There's a book entitled *When Helping You Is Hurting Me* by Carmen Rene Berry. The title pretty much sums up what we need to avoid. If you're like the rest of us you don't like to be hurt, and there are some things you can do to avoid putting yourself in the path of pain—*since most pain is self-induced.* If you go about it the right way you can work on win-win solutions and avoid the heartache.

Devotion is most delicate when it's subtle and you don't even know you're devoted to something. It's a form of subliminal seduction most common when you're succumbing to peer pressure while trying to fit in with a group. Subconsciously you believe the group keeps you safe and secure. But, unfortunately, deep down inside, you need to be part of the group to boost your self-esteem. Far too many blindly follow the crowd and do things they know they shouldn't do, and may not even want to do, all because they're clinging to something *outside* which falsely makes them feel more secure *inside*. It's a sad state of affairs because the bottom line is they're basically following a crowd of followers. Of course, those who have no sense of direction shouldn't be followed under any circumstances. When there's no true leader to be found—*a leader being someone who is a champion for a noble cause*—you'll ultimately end up in a place where you don't want to be.

Question: *What are you devoted to?* Moreover, *why are you devoted to what you're devoted to?* Those two questions may not have compelling answers and don't be too alarmed if your answers make no sense at all; however, when answering those questions, you may feel emotions bubbling from your heart. It's in your best interest if those emotions are positive and everyone involved benefits.

Devotion is joined at the hip with emotion, which can make it extremely rewarding or extremely destructive. How many times have you heard the response *I did it because of love?* The result of doing it in the name of love can be good, bad or downright hideous; therefore, as President Reagan was fond of saying, *trust, buy verify*. For your spiritual well-being keep an open heart, but be vigilant, because your devotion may put you in a position where you'll put *everything* on the line. In extreme cases some individuals become zombies and will sacrifice life and limb for the most inane reasons.

Since this concept is so important, we're going to do something which may change the course of your life immediately. At this time we're going to evaluate everything you're devoted to. Write down every person, organization, concept or ideology that you're making sacrifices for. Of course, you may have thought something was worthwhile in the beginning, only to be shocked and shamed at a later moment. Well, believe it or not, you're not the only one—*and it may not be the last time*. We've all been duped at least once. However, by committing your devotions to paper, we can start the process of putting everything in proper perspective to avoid wasting valuable time.

As an exercise, find a blank sheet of paper and make five columns. In column one write down *what I'm devoted to*. You need to be crystal clear where you are putting your heart and soul. You can't delude yourself into believing it's an honorable cause if it isn't.

In column two write down *why I'm devoted.* Is it for the right reasons or the wrong reasons? Maybe it makes you feel better about yourself because you're giving of yourself, which is a noble thing to do. If you don't feel good about it, there's a problem.

In column three write down *who benefits.* Is your involvement beneficial to everyone concerned? Are you adding value? Are you serving a purpose? If you're giving time, effort and resources there should be a positive result somewhere to be found.

In column four write down *how do I benefit.* What are you getting for the sacrifice of your time and effort? Your blood, sweat and tears need to be rewarded, whether it's financial reward, spiritual reward or something between the two. The something for nothing days must come to a screeching halt.

In column five write down *is it worth it?* The answer must be *yes.* If it's not, it's time to make a change and get a life.

Now start filling in the columns to the best of your ability. It may take some serious effort, but it is well worth the time. The exercise is designed to determine whether you are investing or wasting the precious time you're spending.

If there's too much pain or aggravation associated with any of your devotions, your spirit will be caught in a bird trap. You may feel bottled up, regretful, disenchanted, disillusioned, maybe even resentful and angry. It's really painful when you think about it and ultimately you will remain in pain as long as you allow yourself to be deluded or seduced. It may be deep pain causing you to sink into depression. Even worse, the pain could be subtle where you become accustomed to it, believing that it's the *normal* way you should feel.

For example, years ago a friend of mine, Sarah, was completely devoted to making her relationship work. She is beautiful, intelligent, educated, and everyone loves her; but, unfortunately, the tide turned on her personal relationship and it slipped into negativity. She had every opportunity to walk away from the man she thought she loved, but she wouldn't. Sarah wasn't physically or mentally threatened, yet there was no way she could find her power zone and realize her Dynamic Destiny. All of her family and friends were telling her how crazy she was to hang in there; nonetheless, she kept on trying to make it work while her other half refused to give maximum effort. Sarah became accustomed to the negativity and thought everything was cool. She felt that plenty of people had endured much worse, so she could hang in there a little while longer. Sure, she was correct, but it was crystal clear that she deserved much, much better.

Sarah's devotion was strong which was very admirable. She was committed to making her relationship work, although it was painful. The pain was subtle; she wasn't in imminent danger; she was able to function on a day-to-day basis; and she maintained her sanity. With those considerations in mind, it was obvious Sarah didn't realize she was in pain.

If you've been in love before you know how cyclical it can be. Some of the things we do for the sake of love can be insane, such as convincing ourselves that it ain't really that bad when the relationship starts to sour. That seems to be what Sarah did. Her situation wasn't bad enough to cause her to crash and burn, yet it wasn't good enough to help her take off and fly. She was simply stuck in neutral with pain resonating through every aspect of her life. Every time she decided to move in a new and exciting direction, pain was there to put up a roadblock.

Was Sarah's *devotion* and *sacrifice* worth it? The jury is still out on that one, but to everyone's delight she eventually found the courage to move on. Sarah is now devoted to a relationship with a gentleman who shares her dreams. Equally as important, she's found someone who brings out the best in her and she smiles all the time. She now understands the pain she was in, in her previous relationship, and she's vowed never to travel down that road again. Everyone is proud of the strength she exhibited and pleased to see her realizing her Dynamic Destiny.

About 20 years ago I worked for a real estate company that sold undeveloped land in Florida. I believed all the company hype and attempted to sell to dear friends and colleagues. Fortunately I was a horrible salesman—*I really stunk up the place*—and no one bought any land from me. Yet I was devoted to the company to the point where I sacrificed my free time and energy. I would go in every evening after my day job on a part-time basis. It was physically exhausting and I put a great toll on my body. I put my reputation on the line that what I was selling was legit, but since I wasn't making any money I eventually quit the job, running away like a dog with its tail between its legs.

A couple of months after I quit there was an exposé about how the company I formerly represented was duping investors out of millions of dollars. Sadly the company went belly up and many people in the organization were prosecuted. It was a total disgrace. For quite some time I would hear things like, *hey Kirk, weren't you working for them, selling that bogus land down in Florida?* I had no clue the company wasn't legit. I truly believed in what I was doing, but I didn't do my homework. Had I been paying more attention maybe I would have seen that I put my heart and soul into an organization that was a big charade. Was my devotion worth it? No way. But, on the positive side, I learned the hard way that you've got to pay attention to what you're devoted to; and the more emotion you have invested, the easier it is to be duped. Keep your eyes and ears open and study the obvious. It'll save you a lot of time and a heckuva lot of heartache.

Which way do you go after you've been duped and led astray? Let's be for real—*after you've deluded yourself and allowed yourself to be led astray?* Again, don't beat up on yourself, but we've gotta keep it real. You may feel you were made a fool of or you may ask *how could I have been so stupid?* It's a natural feeling, but you've got to get over it.

Let's look at a positive example of devotion, a true archetype of excellence and one of my heroes, Nelson Mandela. Through his dedication he sacrificed something that he will never recapture— *years of his time and personal freedom.* He was willing to make the sacrifice because he dared to confront human injustice in his homeland. During most of his life South Africa was caught in the throes of apartheid, a rigid policy of segregation of the nonwhite population. Mandela was fierce and totally devoted to fight against it.

In 1962, at the age of 44, Mandela was put in jail and subjected to hard labor in a lime quarry. For a long period of time he was allowed only one letter and one visitor every six months. Through it all, he found a way to earn a Bachelor of Laws degree from the University of London, through its External Programme. In 1985, after 23 years behind bars, he was offered a conditional release from prison if he denounced force as a means to acquire liberation. Mandela declined the offer. Although he was a man of peace, he stood by his conviction that armed struggle is sometimes a necessary option for subjugated and abused people.

Finally, under heavy international political pressure, Mandela was released from prison. One of the most glorious moments in history was watching him stride out of Victor Verster Prison on February 11, 1990. His triumphant walk from the prison grounds was broadcast around the world. He spent 27 years behind bars because he was devoted to the virtues of freedom and equality for his people. To this day his intrepidity and integrity continue to inspire multitudes around the globe. And, by the way, Mandela was elected leader of the very same nation that imprisoned him. In an election open to all people of South Africa, he ascended to the presidency in 1994.

Nelson Mandela is undoubtedly devotion in motion. All that he did was by choice. No one put a gun to his head to be a freedom fighter. He knew exactly what he was devoted to; he knew why he was devoted; he knew exactly who would benefit; and, obviously, it was all worth it. Above all, he was ready, willing and able to sacrifice everything for what he believed in. Ain't no doubt about it, he was and is the man.

With devotion the word *sacrifice* must be clearly understood. Sacrifice means to give up something for the greater good. For your personal well-being sacrifice should not morph into *self-sacrifice* where you short-circuit your self-development and toss all of your dreams to the wind. It's best to make self-development your priority because it will keep you on course to *live in the power zone* and realize your Dynamic Destiny. Accordingly, never lose the *real you*—your *beauty*, your *uniqueness,* your *essence*—in your devotion to any cause. You owe it to yourself to be the incredible person that you are.

In the end make sure that your devotions enable you to become part of something special where everyone walks away with a smile and fond memories. One last thing to think about: *What cause are you willing to devote yourself to you, which is a win-win solution for all involved, as you work on your self-development to realize your Dynamic Destiny?*

# DETERMINATION

*When was the last time that you attempted to do something and you refused to give up?*

*The only way to live the life you want to live is to be determined and not let anything stand in your way, especially self-imposed limitations.*

*F*or some insightful and intelligent reason *The Good Book* instructs us to study ants. Proverbs 6:6-8 says...

*Go to the ant, you sluggard; consider its ways and be wise! It has no commander, no overseer or ruler, yet it stores its provisions in summer and gathers its food at harvest.*

The next time you have the opportunity, take a close look at some ants. Notice how ants are always on the move and they always appear to be dead serious about what they're doing. Ants were created with an innate sense of urgency; consequently they don't play around and they don't waste time. If you put something in front of an ant, watch how it doesn't wait for you to move it out of the way. The ant immediately tries to go around it. If it can't go around it, it tries to go over it or under it. Nature has hard-wired the ant to always give maximum effort to carry out its agenda. They're like the Energizer Bunny—*they just keep going and going and going.* But the real beauty of the ant is that it won't stop trying. You literally must kill an ant to stop it. How would your life be different if you were determined as an ant in pursuit of your dreams and the realization of your Dynamic Destiny?

Throughout the course of your life you will probably be knocked down or maybe even knocked out for a moment in time. At least once you'll be hit below the belt or even sucker punched. Since bad things sometimes happen to good people, it's highly advisable to always be vigilant. Keep your eyes and ears open because you never know what's going to happen. You may have to endure some serious pain to get through the day. Nonetheless, what if every time you crashed to the canvas a vision of an ant flashed through your mind?

An ant would surely appreciate one of my favorite musical artists, Michael Franks, who wrote a song entitled *Never Say Die.* As Michael so eloquently sang...

*Never say die, we've got the worst behind us...*
*If we just try, soon we'll be feeling strong...*
*Cancel our frowns, somehow the light will find us...*
*Can't keep us down, well at least not for long.*

What will it take for you to be determined like an ant? For some reason, as human-beings, we don't have the ant's mentality planted in our brains. The ant was programmed not to quit. It couldn't quit even if it wanted to. If you ripped an ant's leg off it's not going to cry and complain and run to the nearest ant hospital. Rather, it's going to get up, dust itself off and keep on keepin' on to the best of its ability. But, as a human-being, you can do things a little differently because you possess *the power of choice*. With that power you have the ignominious option of caving in. You can just throw your hands up in the air and scream *I don't give a doggone, I quit*. Choice is your prerogative and it can be a blessing or a curse.

In other instances, with the power of choice you can make intelligent decisions and operate on a super-high, intellectual, emotional and spiritual level. You can do some miraculous things, all because you *choose* to keep fighting in the face of adversity. The bottom line is the power of choice, by far, is your most versatile weapon. It must be exercised wisely and used to your best advantage. With that in mind, throughout this chapter you will be asked to invoke the power of choice to move forward with every ounce of fire and passion you have in your body.

The first choice you must make is to *eliminate certain influences from your life*. Number one on my hit list is negative people. Get rid of 'em—they're nauseating. I don't care what you have to do, avoid 'em like the plague. They serve no useful purpose in your life. And who are those dastardly negative people? It's not just those who criticize everything you're attempting to do and tell you you're never going to make it. It's not those obnoxious and cynical jerks predicting total disaster for all mankind. Obviously you should get away from them—*you know better than that.*

The negative people you must be concerned with are those who don't believe in your dream and don't share your vision. Their form of negativity is wily and slowly slithers into your soul, leaving a slime of decay. It can be so subtle and seductive that you probably won't see it, feel it or hear it. It could be sitting across the table from you while using the most eloquent and charming language. It could be staring at you with a glow in its eyes and a beautiful smile. It could make you fall so madly in love that you could literally be sleeping with the enemy. That kind of negativity is a highly infectious disease that you must always defend yourself against. If you let your guard down you can be getting your groove on and all of a sudden your groove comes to a screeching halt. You probably won't know why and your spirit could be broken beyond repair.

Let's say you started a jogging program, but on one particular day you found it difficult to maintain a decent pace. You were really struggling to make every step and it felt like your feet were in cement. But, the next day, when you ran with a group, you instantly had more pep in your step. Your strides were longer and stronger. As your adrenaline started to pump, your endorphins kicked, and you glided on a runner's high. No one put a gun to your head and forced you to jog with more enthusiasm, but for some uncanny reason the group lifted you up into your power zone.

As you may have guessed, negative people who don't share or understand your dream have the exact opposite effect on you. They are the people who see you jogging, watch you exert the necessary effort to move into your power zone, and then they ask, *"Dude, why are you jogging? Why are you worried about staying in shape, it's too hot out there? Are you a fool?"* Of course, they're not consciously trying to discourage you; they're just expressing opinions based on lack of vision. They don't understand you, nor do they understand why you're doing what you're doing. You're pushing and grinding to be the best you can be and they just don't get it because they're not with the program. They're nice people, great members of the community, good friends and maybe even family members who love and adore you. They are people who may have your best interest at heart—*at least in their minds*—but they can assassinate your spirit and your dream. They can set up a roadblock between you and your Dynamic Destiny—*but only if you allow them to!*

On the other hand, what if you jog by and you were cheered? It's a hot, hazy, humid day; you're falling apart and you want to cash in the chips; but, someone encouraged you to keep pushing forward. You're inspired, so you continue onward through the pain, but then you fall on your face in the dirt. That same person helps you get up, dusts you off and encourages you to pick up the pace with a swift kick in the rear end for an extra jolt of energy. Before you know it, you reach the finish line. Obviously that individual sees something positive in you and understands what you're accomplishing. With that in mind, the second choice to make is to *get around positive people.* When times are tough they will undoubtedly be your saving grace.

For instance, I've been through tough emotional and economic times over the last decade. My business ventures were hit hard by the subprime crisis and I have writhed in the wind of financial turmoil far beyond my imagination. Through it all my best and oldest buddy in the world, Gary, has always been a positive voice. He understands my trials and tribulations and he's always seen the light, as dim as it may be. The interesting thing is he never *tries* to be positive, he simply *is* positive. I can honestly say I've never heard him utter anything negative or discouraging about me or my situation. Honestly, I don't think he has the mental composition to do so. If I've screwed everything up and I feel like manure, after speaking to him I see things in a positive light and I feel far better—*and I'm more determined than ever.*

Those individuals who have the innate ability *to see the good side* are few and far between. While many see problems, they see challenges; and then they help you see solutions! Unquestionably they are the people you need to hang around and keep as your confidants. There's no doubt about it, those kinds of friendships will steer you through choppy waters. Essentially they are priceless. In my case it's especially true, considering that Gary is the person who introduced me to *Think & Grow Rich* by Napoleon Hill back in our college days. It's undoubtedly the most prolific self-help book ever written and it's a major part of my life. That introduction ignited a passion in me which will never be extinguished; hence, we are together right now, moving you into your power zone and plotting the realization of your Dynamic Destiny.

The key to getting around positive people is for you to exude positivity with the people you come in contact with. If you do so you will become a magnet for positive people who will want to be around you. Essentially you attract the type of person that you are. Those who are attempting to realize their dreams are always craving for inspiration. Obviously you will have internal bouts with negativity, cynicism and maybe even self-loathing from time to time, but those moments will be brief when a positive mental attitude is at your core. As long as you're a wellspring of encouragement for others in need, before you know it you'll be around nothing but positive people. You will feed off their energy and they will thrive off yours.

Years ago I was in a golf tournament in Florida. There was a gentleman there that I'd always wanted to do business with by the name of Willie Gary. Willie is one of the most successful litigation attorneys in the world and he's won many major court battles. To top it off he's a very inspiring individual. During one of the tournament festivities

I walked up to him and introduced myself. We spoke all of 15 seconds before he was bombarded by others seeking his attention. The next day I saw him during lunch after a round of golf and I was sure he had forgotten we met. Much to my surprise he recognized me and sat down right next to me. I was shocked. Willie could have easily sought the company of someone he knew well, but he decided to break bread with little ole me. Of course, that says the world about him—*and how lucky I was!* As successful as he's become he doesn't forget the little people, which is one of the traits of a truly positive person. It's no wonder he's so successful.

As we were eating I asked Willie how did he take off and what was his key for success? For 45 precious minutes I got a firsthand account of his life story. His eloquence and spirit sent my motivation level through the roof. He convinced me that I could and would succeed, if I set my mind to it. Willie said the key to his success was *there comes a point when ya gotta step out on faith.* There was no magic to it, you just have to believe and fight through the tough times. That conversation was a turning point in my life. I was infected by his positivity and I became a believer. I left our lunch table more determined than ever to do whatever it takes to realize my

Dynamic Destiny. Since that moment my greatest undertaking is to pass positivity on to the next person who needs an injection.

It may take a while to attract more positive people into your life, so be patient. Between now and then the positive voices currently in your life may not be loud or strong enough to at least counter the negative voices. It makes life especially tough when you're behind the eight ball and under immense stress and strain. In those moments, if you are not of strong conviction, the negative voices grow louder and louder and reverberate through the chambers of your mind. The louder they grow, the heavier the weight upon your shoulders. Then, before you know it, the burden is too much to bear and your back breaks—*you quit.* Again, the folks behind those voices aren't negative people per se, they're just not working in your best interest; therefore, don't allow their lack of vision to obscure your view. In those situations where you feel your life imploding, whatever you do, don't despair. As difficult as it may be, maintain a spirit of optimism and remain focused on your goal. If you do so the positive voices will become stronger and keep you determined.

To be fair there are those who sometimes become more motivated by the naysayers. They thrive on proving people wrong, but they're the exception. Those types are very strong-willed and have the ability to totally shut out the rest of the world when necessary. No doubt about it, they are definitely to be admired. Most of us fall prey to the subterfuge of the world and succumb to its temptations. Far too many cave in to peer pressure and the negative influence of those we associate with. That being the tendency, when necessary you must be exceptionally disciplined to extricate yourself from negative people and negative environments.

The third choice you must make is to *look for every possible way to succeed, while being flexible.* Recall the ant which looks for an alternate route if you put something in front of it. The ant can do that because it doesn't fall prey to tunnel vision. It's not sucked into one way of thinking or acting. Accordingly, don't feel you must succeed in the exact way you originally set out to succeed. If an ant can and must find an alternate route, surely you can.

What if you had driving directions to get to a party, but on one of the roads there was a traffic jam. Would you just sit there feeling powerless or would you venture off and find another route? Being determined to reach your destination the way originally planned is an admirable thing, but being *flexible* and *adaptable* will lift your game to a higher level. *Flexibility* illuminates other avenues of opportunity, while *adaptability* clarifies an ever changing environment. Taking it a step further, sometimes it's necessary to scrap your entire plan and improvise to get the job done. As you become more and more determined you simply do what you've got to do.

Finally, let's examine the old Yogi Berra aphorism *it ain't over 'til it's over.* I don't know if you play golf, but the last time I played it all came down to the last whole. In golf you play eighteen holes and for seventeen of the eighteen I was stinkin' up the place and embarrassing myself. But I kept whispering in my mind, *hang in there...it ain't over 'til it's over...you still have a chance...there's still opportunity*; then came the last hole. Everyone in my group missed the green and I hit my ball 15 feet from the cup. I birdied the hole and saved my entire round. Unfortunately there were other times when I didn't hang in there. I remember once giving up half-way through the round because I was so far down I thought I could never come back. But I'll never feel that way again, because *it ain't over 'til it's over.* If you maintain relentless determination through the toughest times, combined with optimism, you may find that a window of opportunity pops open when you least expect it.

If we read between the lines of the aphorism *it ain't over 'til it's over* we would find that equanimity is the name of the game. Simply put, it's staying cool under pressure. The real deal is, while in the process of taking your life to the next level, you're going to be in precarious situations. Many of them can't be avoided or predicted, so you've gotta deal with them like a champion. You will be beat up mentally, physically and spiritually, but as long as there's the slightest possibility you can come out on top—as long as you don't fear defeat—as long as you're willing to do whatever it takes to get the job done—as long as you believe in your God-given talent—if you simply maintain equanimity, your determination could squeeze you through the door of success.

The next time you're knocked down remember your old friend the ant. It just won't quit and neither will you. When necessary you will get up off the canvas, time and time again. Question: *How determined are you prepared to be, through the toughest challenges of your life, to realize your Dynamic Destiny?*

# DISCIPLINE

*What little thing or small task are you disciplined enough to do, each and every day, whether it's mundane, painful, exciting or exhilarating, which is moving you closer to your ultimate goal?*

*It's the little things in life that count. The weight of a little snowflake is barely perceptible, but don't get caught in a snow storm.*

*T*o realize your Dynamic Destiny you must make a life-changing decision: *Will you overcome the pain of discipline or suffer the pain of regret?* During the course of your life you will wrestle with both of those pains. Pain is a necessary part of life and there's simply no way around it, so you may as well get used to it; and the higher your goals and aspirations, the more pain you must endure. The option for which pain you want to engage is now on the table. If you choose the pain of discipline you will actually deal with growing pains. Something tells me that's exactly what you're craving. By not choosing the pain of discipline, by default, you are inviting the pain of regret to meticulously take root in your life. Keep in mind that regret will most likely be accompanied by unimaginable stagnation and degradation. Something tells me that ain't what you want.

You've probably met an old, sarcastic and cynical person in your travels. I'd bet, in some way or another, the pain of regret killed him emotionally. He decided years ago that discipline wasn't his thing; it just wasn't what he was all about. By refusing to do what he could and should have done years ago, he became prey to be hunted down by regret. Eventually it caught him by the tail, then stagnation and degradation slowly started to devour him. That process can be manifested by a bankrupt spirit, ill health, poverty, deteriorated relationships, ignorance, irresponsibility and a long list of other ugly maladies.

The beauty of the pain of discipline is clear to see. If you play your cards right and do what you *know* you're supposed to do, when you're supposed to do it, the pain of discipline will magically mature into the joy of achievement. Discipline takes you down a grueling path that will become a pleasant ride over the course of time. The problem arises when you expect a pleasant ride, down an easy path, to begin your journey of success. It ain't happenin' unless you get real lucky; therefore, it's vital to understand and visualize what could possibly happen when the correct path is chosen. Odds are that path will appear painful and laborious at first glance, but you must continually visualize the beauty of the final destination and keep that in the forefront of your mind.

If you look up the word discipline in the dictionary you will find *training expected to produce a specific character or pattern of behavior, especially training that produces moral or mental improvement.* By that definition there's no doubt that *discipline* is the magic word for personal achievement and dare I say it will *guarantee* success. Your success may not be exactly how you initially visualized it, but at the very least something positive and powerful will be your end result. Whether you realize it or not, through discipline you have the magic wand in your hand to pull the rabbit out of the hat.

You've probably figured out by now that you can take any one of the Dynamic Destiny concepts we've uncovered thus far, and with complete focus on that sole concept, you would have enough firepower to rise like cream to the top and *live in the power zone*. To this point we've discussed dreams, desires, decisions, devotion and determination, but discipline is the sole concept which will *guarantee* positive results. The other concepts may sometimes go awry and hurl you into negative circumstances and effects.

For example, let's say your *dream* propels you to take action. Of course, taking action is the key to making your dream come true, but the action you take could be haphazard and foolish or the dream may be unrealistic. Let's say you have great *desire* and you're completely focused. Desire is potent and can be dangerous, especially if you cross the wrong lines to quench your thirst. Let's say you finally made a major *decision* regarding the direction of your life. You did your due diligence to the best of your ability, but you missed a step and your decision produced nothing but tumult. Maybe there was a time when you were totally *devoted* to a virtuous cause. You worked hard and long with a great group of like-minded individuals, but you were too blind to see the cause was a total charade and you ended up completely devastated. Lastly, what if you are *determined* to do whatever it takes to get the job done and you receive all of the accolades of success. You get up early and stay up late, but the cost of success was too much and your result was a Pyrrhic victory. In those scenarios it's easy to see how each concept can go completely haywire, if its application is somewhat misdirected.

The virtue of discipline seems to be a completely different story. There doesn't appear to be a negative consequence of discipline—*and in this sense we're talking about self-discipline.* Discipline means to be completely focused on a destination, while being diligent and patient enough to endure the growing pains to reach it. That translates into disciplined people understanding what they want in the *long term.* For them the short term is just a series of events or checkpoints that influence and build up to the long term.

Undisciplined people can only see into the next day, week or month. With limited or distorted foresight they take actions today which could produce disastrous results in the future. Oftentimes they have no clue of the consequences of their actions because they *refuse* to look ahead, while operating like an ostrich with its head in the sand. Their mantra is *what 'cha don't know won't hurt 'cha.* Contrary to popular belief, what you don't know or refuse to see can hurt you—*it can even kill you.* Make no mistake about it that the refusal to look ahead is a self-fulfilling prophecy for a damned future.

On the other hand disciplined people vividly imagine a crystal clear future they desire to bring into reality. What they imagine is usually years, even decades away, all due to their extraordinary long term vision. They then import the future they imagine into their present lifestyles, which fortifies their discipline and keeps them on the path of success. And to make it even sweeter, they are able to infuse discipline into all of the other Dynamic Destiny concepts to insure they are not abused. So,

with that in mind, is it possible to be *too disciplined?*
I don't think so.

Once I was in Central Park in Manhattan, which is
my favorite place to go jogging. There was a
gentleman I knew, Hank, grossly out of shape, barely
able to move. In fact, I thought he was walking
when he said he was jogging; but, he was out there
anyway, giving it all he had. Hank's goal was to
make it one time around Central Park. He told me,
*"One day I'll be able to do it, I'll just take it nice and
slow and easy, but I will get there."* I thought to
myself it ain't looking too good right now, Hank. I
was fearful he might kill himself trying to get in
shape? But Hank had serious motivation. His
doctor told him to lose some weight or else. The *or
else* scared him so much he had to take action.

About six months later I saw Hank in the park and
unmistakably he was jogging. He must have shed 45
to 50 pounds and he looked like a powerful stallion,
so much so that at first glance I didn't recognize
him. When we spoke he told me he started out only
able to jog $1/10^{th}$ of a mile before his fuel tank was
depleted. He was so upset with himself he decided
to jog every day, regardless of the weather, so he
could one day make it around Central Park. And,

by the way, Central Park is a tough six mile trek. It can break you down mentally and physically if you're not prepared. At the time we spoke he said he was finally able to make it around the park and he had set a goal to run a marathon.

There's no doubt in my mind that Hank will one day conquer a 26-mile marathon because he understands one of the keys to his success—*the ability to look into the future with clarity.* He could visualize himself one day kicking out 26 miles, provided he's disciplined enough to do what is necessary to get the job done. He also said, *"At first my strides were painful, but now they're becoming pleasurable, and I feel like a champion!"* It's amazing what a little discipline will do.

The real deal is that Hank was able to deal with the monotony and growing pains between $1/10^{th}$ of a mile and six miles. There were some days that he didn't want to get out of the bed, but he pushed himself. He found the key to running every day was to make it the first thing he did. Hank would get out of bed, put on his running attire, put a little food in his belly and hit the road. There was nothing to think about, he just did it. He also kept in mind there was no need to rush. He wasn't running with anyone else at a faster pace, which could have caused him to burn out and become frustrated. Hank ran at his own pace and he did his own thing. He knew that it would take a long time to build the stamina to reach six miles, but he was willing to take baby steps until he developed the power and grace to take full strides. All he had to do was accept the toll to pay— *the pain of discipline*—which really is a small price considering how much pleasure he was being rewarded with on the back end.

Check this one out: How much money would you have if you doubled a penny every year for the next thirty years? You have to admit, a penny is such a small amount, why would we even want to discuss it? Well the answer is $10,737,418.24. That's a lot of money from just one little penny. The point is undisciplined people would view the question from how long it takes. Thirty years is such a long time away that they wouldn't even entertain the question. To the contrary, a disciplined individual would think it's an intriguing question and what is the meaning behind it? He'd pull out a calculator, find that it is ten million-plus dollars, get excited and start thinking about how it applies to his life. He'd think sure, it's a long way off, but in the grand scheme of life, it really ain't. Then he'd implement some type of plan to make it all happen. His plan may be modified and may not even include ten million dollars, but his long-term thinking process would be ignited and something positive would be set in motion.

Disciplined people understand the journey toward personal achievement doesn't happen overnight. They specialize and know how to *grind it out.* That means they have the mental fortitude to do whatever it takes, on each particular day, although what they do may not show any obvious signs of progress in the beginning. They're even prepared to take a few steps backward so they can take giant steps forward in the future. Disciplined people don't complain and they don't become anxious in the process of realizing their dreams. An undisciplined person is uptight and always thinking *I gotta get there...I gotta hurry up and get there.* But the disciplined person is thinking *there ain't no rush...if I keep doin' what I'm doin' it's just a matter of time before it all comes together.*

In 1997 Tiger Woods won the biggest golf tournament in the world, the Masters. Not only did he win it, he set all kinds of records in the process and thoroughly beat down his opponents. His victory was unprecedented and we may never see another performance on par with it. During that year he also won three other tournaments and became the number one golfer in the world, all at age 21. For the average golfer that was a miraculous year, but it wasn't good enough for Tiger—*he was thirsty for more.*

To quench his thirst for a better golf game in 1998 Tiger decided he had to change his swing. Everybody thought he was a fool and he was trashed by his critics, but Tiger's thinking was on a completely different plane. The pundits asked, *Tiger, why would you change something that worked so well, which enabled you to dominate your opponents?* Tiger's sentiment was simply *I have more in me.*

In 1998 he suffered mightily because of his conviction to make a positive change. He only won one tournament. Most professional golfers would take one victory and be very happy with it, but for Tiger it was a disappointment. Everybody thought he lost the Midas touch and he was doomed to crash and burn. Nevertheless he was devoted and determined to make the changes he thought were necessary to improve his golf swing and enable him to dominate the game at an even higher level. But that devotion and determination didn't mean a thing without the discipline he was able to maintain throughout the process. He wouldn't go back to the golfer he was. He flat out refused to.

Tiger worked relentlessly, day after day, doing the little things no one else would do, which make the big difference. It took more than a year of painstaking effort before he called his coach one day and said the magic words, *"I got it."* What he was working on finally clicked in and could then be used in the heat of battle. The only reason *he got it* was because he had the ability to maintain mental control to continue to do what was necessary, in the face of violent criticism. As a consequence, at the point at which *he got it*, he was able to do things no one thought was humanly possible on a golf course. Tiger's success is all about discipline, make no mistake about it. He was strong enough to take baby steps and accept the growing pains associated with discipline. Now he enjoys the pleasure of possessing the greatest golf game the world has ever seen. Tiger's discipline has made him a living legend in the world of golf.

The Chinese bamboo tree has the word discipline written all over it. The first year its mighty seed is planted you'll be lucky to see a little bulb popping out of the ground. You can water it as much as you want, pray and chant, and that's about all you'll get. Indeed, for the next three years you may be extremely disappointed by its lack of progress. Of course, any sane person would wonder if the doggone thing is going to pop up out of the ground and realize its full potential. But, lo and behold, in year five it shoots up 80 to 90 feet, a truly amazing feat. The Chinese bamboo tree is a very patient plant and it's disciplined enough to grow underground for four years. No one can see what it's doing, but it's putting in the necessary labor for success. It spreads its roots and lays a firm foundation upon which to grow tall and strong. Then it simply shoots up to unbelievable heights.

During years one through four I'd bet all the other plants in the garden made fun of it and doubted whether or not it had the guts to grow and succeed. And, you know what, the same thing may happen to you when you decide to become disciplined. Family and friends will think you're crazy, you're too serious, you're working too hard, you're never going to make it—*essentially you're a fool.* But *you* must believe when no one else will.

When you're disciplined you may be forced to stand alone and accept the pain everyone else fears. Many outside forces will lose faith in you quickly if they don't see progress immediately. It's their loss, not yours, because you know the pain will turn to pleasure if you stay on course. Never fear standing alone because it will make you much stronger and much wiser. As important, it will also let you know who is in your corner at crunch time.

Now that we know discipline is the magic word, how do we attract it into our lives? How do we do what we need to do, when we need to do it, while enjoying the process? There are three simple keys for a disciplined life which you must take to heart. First and most important, you must *keep your end result in mind*. You must be able to see your target, even if it doesn't physically exist. Operating without light at the end of the tunnel can short-circuit the average person's discipline and subconsciously induce a failure mentality. To maintain discipline self-induced illumination must be your guiding light.

Second, to invoke discipline you must *create a sense of urgency*. Undisciplined people are masters of procrastination and they never really push themselves to get the job done. Pushing yourself when you're not forced to is one of the toughest things in the world to do. It's so easy to lay back and do less than what is necessary, especially when there's no *direct* punishment for being lazy. But, for disciplined people, their sense of urgency is their motivation— *they want to get it on.* They don't need pain or force to get them to move. Disciplined people convince themselves what needs to be done needs to be jumped on right now. They understand the consequences of not taking action are severe, even if the severity can't be detected in the present moment. And let's not mistake a sense of urgency with rushing the process of success. A sense of urgency is extremely powerful, but the virtue of patience should never be overlooked.

As an example, imagine you're going on vacation for a week, you have a 7:00 a.m. flight tomorrow morning, and of course you have a million things to do before leaving. You'd probably make a prioritized list of what needs to be done and immediately jump on it. You wouldn't let anything distract you because the flight tomorrow will leave with or without you. That 7:00 a.m. deadline is sharp, not soft, and it creates a sense of urgency that motivates you.

From this point forward, manufacture your own sense of urgency by creating deadlines for yourself. You don't want to miss that flight in the morning because you will suffer. You'll probably have to pay a premium fare to catch a flight later in the day, if you can get a flight at all. And then, to top it off, your wife looks at you like you're an idiot—*trust me, I know.* I've missed my fair share of flights. That being said, when creating deadlines there must be pain associated with it if you blow it. You can think *oh well, if I don't get it done by x, y, z time, it's okay...there's always tomorrow.* That ain't workin'. You have to be a little harder on yourself.

The third key to pull discipline into your life is to *make what you need to do your first task of the day.* When you get out of the bed immediately jump on the task at hand. Don't even think about it, just do it, just like Hank jumped out of bed and started running. Doing it first creates a positive habit. Bad habits are hard to break and good habits are hard to make, but it's easier to make good habits stick when they come before anything else you do. There is far less tendency to be thrown off track and fewer temptations to battle.

For instance, let's say you're starting a new exercise program. You decide you're going to exercise every day, right after work, at six o'clock p.m. Well, what if there's an emergency at work and you have to pull a little over-time? The later you stay at work and the more tired you become, the greater the tendency to skip your workout, go home, eat, drink and crash. On the contrary, when you get started early—*let's say six a.m. instead of six p.m.*—there are way fewer distractions at that hour. Odds are you won't be called to come to work early compared to staying late. Also, when you start early, you're much more fresh and invigorated, as opposed to being battle weary at the end of the day. Sure, some people are *early* people, some people are *late* people, but most successful people attack the day early. Once a gentleman told me if I wanted to meet with him I'd have to be in his office at 7:00 a.m., no exceptions. I thought he was crazy, but when I got to his office he was on fire and making things happen. Early people are like the army, *they do more by 10:00 a.m. than most people do all day.*

So now you have the keys to a disciplined life. All you have to do is keep your end result in mind, create a sense of urgency and get started early. There are probably a million other ways to get the job done, but at least you have a sound start. Don't be tempted to take the easy way out, because the road to a successful life is never easy. Be tough on yourself and life won't be tough on you. Accept the pain of discipline and you'll never suffer from the pain of regret.

One last question: *What disciplined effort will you undertake on a daily basis, which the average man will forego, that may be painful at first, but will produce a lifetime of pleasure and joy, which will guarantee the manifestation of your Dynamic Destiny?*

# DARING

*Are you gutsy enough to take the dare to live the life of your dreams?*

*The late, great jazz musician Miles Davis was featured on a billboard ad with the caption* Dare to be Different. *Sometimes just being* different *is all it takes to rise to the top.*

*M*iles Davis was as bold as can be and he always had an aura of fearlessness. His musical career began in the 1940's where he became a star playing with the late be-bop genius Charlie Parker. The *Miles mystique* developed and it is like no other. It continued to grow through the 50's, 60's, 70's, 80's and 90's. Where most great musicians only have one era of dominance, Miles was *the man* for close to 50 years until the day he passed away. What made him so alluring was his ability to adapt to different musical styles and flourish in all of them. He was intrepid when it came to making musical statements and he didn't look back. What he played in the 40's and 50's he refused to play in the 80's and 90's. Miles didn't have a rear view mirror and he always relished the next challenge. Above all else, Miles *dared* to be different, which lifted him to immortal status in the world of music. To realize your Dynamic Destiny and *live in the power zone* you too must be daring— *and the loftier your dreams, the more daring you must be!*

All of the previous Dynamic Destiny concepts we've discussed thus far must be pulled together, synthesized and brought to the surface so you can now *go for it.* Question: *Are you mentally prepared to take the dare, accept the challenge and rise to the occasion?* If you are, buckle up, because there's more fun to be had—*it's time to rock'n'roll!*

Years ago I wrote an article entitled *Striving for Perfection* and I know what you're thinking—I'm never going to be perfect, so why be an idiot and try? Good argument, but I'm not buying it. The premise of *Striving for Perfection* is that perfection is not *sustainable*, but it is *attainable*. Make no mistake about it, perfection can be had. For instance, Don Larson pitched a perfect game in the 1956 World Series. Parker Bohn III bowled more than 80 perfect games in heated Professional Bowlers Association competition. Nadia Comaneci scored multiple perfect 10's in the 1976 Olympic Games. The 1972 Miami Dolphins had an undefeated perfect season en route to winning Super Bowl VII. Rocky Marciano retired as the heavyweight boxing champion in 1956 with a perfect record of 49-0. There were probably times when you were in grade school and got every answer right on a test, getting a perfect score of 100. I'll bet there was a time when you were madly in love and it felt perfect.

It's crystal clear that there is such a thing as perfection. It's out there for you, it's just impossible to stay in the perfection zone forever. Life's rollercoaster unceasingly takes us up and down and around dangerous curves when we decide to go for it. But, of course, the exhilaration and excitement makes the danger all worth it, especially when we venture into that perfection zone every now and then.

If we can agree that perfection is not sustainable, but it is attainable, a huge problem is eliminated. We no longer have to frustrate ourselves by trying to be perfect all the time—*it just ain't happenin'*. We can accept and more importantly learn from our mistakes while continuing to carry on, with the expectation and purpose that our next action will take us deeper into that perfection zone. And when we do hit that slippery and fleeting moment of perfection, we'll have the patience and drive to dare to go for it again and again. We can't hit it once and rest on our laurels. Surely after Nadia Comaneci got her first perfect 10 in the Olympics she wasn't satisfied. She was probably thinking *I just got a perfect 10 yesterday...if I got one, I know I can get another...I think I'll go for it!* She dared to go for it again and again, on the world's largest stage, and she hit the perfection zone six times. It was an unprecedented feat which amazed everyone across the globe.  The question is what exactly must we do to be more and more daring like Nadia so we can score perfect 10's and realize our dreams?

The Dynamic Destiny Principle of *daring* is based on a five-step process of striving for perfection.  It's designed to put you in a mental mindset to go for it again and again.  First, we must overcome our natural fear of looking like a fool.  Second, we must start acting like a fool.  Third, we must develop a level of competence.  Fourth, we must develop a level of expertise.  And fifth, we must fine tune our efforts while we strive for perfection.  Whether we realize it or not, all of those steps come into play whenever we're attempting to become better at whatever it is we attempt to do.  To become more daring and accept more challenges we're going to concentrate on the first two steps.

Step number one:  *Overcome the natural fear of looking like a fool.*  Let's back up for a moment and take a look at the words *natural fear*.  None of us want to look like a fool for fear of criticism or ridicule.  In the classic book *Think and Grow Rich* by Napoleon Hill, the fear of criticism is one of the *Six Ghosts of Fear*, along with the fears of poverty, sickness, old age, death, and loss of love.  In fact,

Napoleon Hill believed that your three main enemies are indecision, doubt and fear. Indecision invites doubt, and they work in conjunction to create fear.

For example, there was a time I was at a party and I noticed a beautiful lady across the room. She wasn't dancing, nor was I, so the table was perfectly set for romance. All I had to do was man up, walk over there and ask her to dance; however, I was indecisive and I began to doubt myself. I thought if I walked over there and asked her to dance and she said no, I would look like a fool and be totally embarrassed. As I debated in my mind whether I should rise to the occasion and stroll on over, some brave gent proudly walked over there and stole my girl. The next thing you know they're out there dancing up a storm and having a grand time. I chickened out and blew an opportunity by allowing my fear of rejection to dominate me—*so much for romance that evening.*

Overcoming your natural fear of looking like a fool really goes back to the first time you attempted to do something and you stumbled. Depending on your mental composition at that time, you may have been completely embarrassed. As a kid it can really be devastating if you're teased by others—*or even as an adult.* So what happens is you develop a fear of going for it. The *natural fear* is not really natural and you're not born with it. It's developed over a period of time and it can be deeply ingrained while infecting everything you attempt to do. Only a small percentage of us break through that fear at an early age, if at all.

Stage fright is a form of the fear of ridicule. Have you ever practiced something over and over again, until you could do it in your sleep, but when the time finally came to do it for real you just froze? Your body locked up and you couldn't pull the trigger and fire. Or, just as bad, you pulled the trigger, but you misfired and choked.

Once during a talent show in my high school there was a duo performing a classic song. The little lady of the duo sang first and she was absolutely beautiful. Anyone could see she was nervous, but she didn't let that stop her from thrilling the crowd. When it was the little gentleman's turn to sing he froze. He was out of tune, out of rhythm and forgot the words of the song. She actually had to whisper the words of the song to him so he could get through the chorus. It was absolutely horrible, still he could sing like a champ walking down the hallway or at the backyard barbeque; but, when *the moment* called for him to step up, he fell down.

To *live in the power zone* you must overcome any fear of ridicule reverberating through your mind and take sanguine strides toward your Dynamic Destiny. Transitioning from fearful to fearless may be a daunting task, but it's the only way to realize your greatness and live the life you deserve. Keeping one simple thought in mind may be your saving grace: *imagine how miserable your life could be if you don't go for it.* Just think about it for a second. We've gone through six steps of the *Dynamic Destiny Principle*, but those steps mean absolutely nothing unless you are daring enough to do what is necessary to make things happen. If you sit back, hesitate, and let fear mentally paralyze you, by default you will leave the door wide open for the Dynamic Duo of *Aggravation* and *Agitation* to happily stroll in. They will sit down at your dining room table, have dinner and zealously plot a life of desperation and despair especially tailored for you. To top it off they will guarantee that undesirable things will happen *to you*, but little of substance and beauty will happen *for you*. Right now, at this moment, you must decide to not allow your life to be destroyed by not going for it.

The late, great John H. Johnson, founder and publisher of *Ebony* and *Jet* magazines, is one of my personal heroes. He wrote something apropos to our discussion in his autobiography, *Succeeding Against the Odds*, which has been embedded in my mind since it was published. For me his sentiments have made all the difference in the world and I always think of him when I'm fearful of pulling the trigger and going for it. Mr. Johnson said...

> *There were two choices, and two choices only before me and I had to choose. The choice, as usual, was between security and insecurity, the known and the unknown. I had to decide whether I was going to hang on to the devil I knew or whether I was going to turn loose, without a safety net, and free fall to danger, destiny, wealth or death. I've believed ever since that living on the edge, living in and through your fear, is the summit of life and that people who refuse to take that dare condemn themselves to a life of living death.*

When you look at it like that it becomes crystal clear—*it's do or die baby!* If you don't go for it your heart will continue to beat, but you may be walking amongst the living dead whose dreams were shattered, all because they were paralyzed by fear. Mr. Johnson went on to say...

*And I'm convinced that the only way to get ahead in this world is to live and sell dangerously. You've got to live beyond your means. You've got to commit yourself to an act or a vision that pulls you further than you want to go and focuses you to use your hidden strengths. For you're stronger than you think you are. And what you need—what all men and women need—is an irrevocable act that forces you, on pain of disgrace, jail or death, to be the best you that you can be.*

Could it possibly be said any better? I never had the pleasure of meeting Mr. Johnson, but it's obvious he knew what he was talking about. Keep in mind those sentiments come from a man who mortgaged his mother's furniture for a few hundred bucks and parlayed it into approximately three hundred million dollars in the magazine publishing industry.

Another roadblock when deciding to go for it can be an inferiority complex. There are countless people who feel they're just not good enough to succeed. They suffer from low self-esteem and consequently pass up opportunities which could catapult them into their dreams. Henry C. Link once wrote *"While one person hesitates because he feels inferior, the other is busy making mistakes and becoming superior."* Whatever you do, don't let an inferiority complex stand between you and your Dynamic Destiny. You were born with everything you need to be successful. Maybe it's all buried deep down inside your soul, but now the time is ripe for excavation.

Once I was on a romantic date with a beautiful lady who could sing wonderfully. We both attended Rutgers University in our younger days and I always thought she had potential to be a professional entertainer. As we were driving in my car all of a sudden a song came on the radio by the sultry soul singer Regina Belle. Regina also went to Rutgers with us and sang her way to stardom. With extreme confidence my date proclaimed, *"I can sing just as good as she can,"* and she proceeded to prove the point, right there in the car. She sang everything Regina sang, note for note, and she sounded spectacular. Sure, she could do it, but did she *have* it?

My date never realized her true singing potential because she didn't *dare* to showcase her talent. She was scared to put it all on the line quite possibly because she felt inferior to the task at hand. Anyone can throw a concert on the New Jersey Turnpike in the passenger seat of a car, but singing to thousands under the heat of a spotlight is a totally different ballgame. Regina was realizing her Dynamic Destiny because she dared to do so, yet, in my date's humble opinion, Regina got real lucky.

What my date and I did agree upon is that Regina is extremely talented. She has a gift that very few have been blessed with. Way before she cut her first CD I vividly remember her singing to a one-man audience, yours truly, in one of the musical practice rooms on campus. I was enthralled and she instantly became one of my favorite singers. It was easy to sense her commitment and drive, which made it obvious that she was the real deal. What my date failed to realize is that Regina's God-given talent would have been a complete waste had she not put it to good use. Regina seized the opportunity to be a phenomenal singer by being gutsy and feeling inferior to no one. Make no mistake about it, if Regina was lucky, it was only because she put herself in a position to be lucky by being daring.

Step two in your quest for perfection is to start acting like a fool. Just jump in there and start making a few mistakes—*take a chance for crying out loud.* Have some fun and start laughing at yourself. You may look like a fool taking a chance, but not in the derogatory sense. It's not because you're an idiot doing something stupid for a dumb reason. What you're doing is engaging in an activity with the purpose of getting better, and to get better you must stumble every once in a while. I once remember a gentleman saying *don't go through it, grow through it.* Get better day-by-day by learning from your mistakes, even if you look a little silly in the process. You probably don't remember, but I'd bet the first time you tried to walk you fell down. Then some loving person picked you up, dusted you off and made you try again and again and again, until you succeeded. Back then you weren't thinking about looking silly or foolish. It's best to adopt that philosophy again.

Once I went skiing and you probably know how dangerous skiing can be. Forget about breaking a leg, you can kill yourself. I was at Hunter Mountain in New York with a friend and we got on the ski lift and kept going up and up and up the mountain. We were on a black diamond trail; and, by the way, black diamond means the toughest slope to ski down. The higher we went up the more nervous I got. Now what an adult might think about skiing down a dangerous slope is *are you a fool? Why in the world would you go skiing and break your leg?* But a kid would think, *wow, let's go skiing. We can have snowball fights and roll around in the snow. It'll be so much fun!*

The kid has little to no concept of the danger associated with the task at hand. He doesn't know he can break his leg or crack a few ribs, consequently he goes skiing and has a ball. And, you guessed it, the adult stays home, watches TV and works on his beer belly. Fear doesn't mentally cripple kids as it cripples adults, which is why kids have so much fun. My friend, who also was an expert skier and happened to be on the ski patrol, said, *"Follow me."* I was foolish enough to follow him with my suspect skiing technique, but I made it down the slope and had a whale of a time. Afterwards my buddy said I could go skiing with him any time all because I took the dare. *(By the way, I'm not advising you to go skiing. It's not a sport for the faint of heart. I've had friends who have actually sustained major injuries doing so. A stroll around the park is certainly a lot safer and maybe even more fun.)*

Once I was on the beach in Jamaica working on my tan. For some reason I decided to take wind surfing lessons to test out my theory of looking like a fool and going for it. Ten years earlier I had taken windsurfing lessons with a group of friends at a lake. As I remember, it was the toughest thing I'd ever tried to do. Back then hardly anyone witnessed me falling off the wind surf and splashing into the water countless times, barely making progress; but, the beach in Jamaica was jam packed. I thought to myself *do you really want to embarrass yourself and look like a fool in front of all these people?* Well, I got up on that wind surf a million times and came crashing down into the water a million times. My feet and hands were sore, my whole body was beat up and only God knows how many gallons of salt water I swallowed. It was one of the most trying experiences I've ever had.

What was most interesting about my windsurfing escapade was that after I'd fallen on my face maybe ten times, I forgot about everyone on the beach watching me. I stopped being self-conscious. It was just me, the instructor, the water and the wind surf. No longer were there a million pairs of eyes judging me and laughing at me. I went into a zone and I wasn't concerned about anything except *going for it.*

My fear of ridicule was gone and I was operating without fear. It was one of the most liberating experiences I've ever had. Another interesting point was later that evening many people came up to me and said I looked great out there, which I couldn't believe. Some said I was brave and patted me on the back. Some admitted they could never take beginner lessons in front of all of those people. At that moment I realized that I should never be Chicken Little again, nor should I fear putting myself in uncomfortable positions.

If you haven't been daring in the past, now is the time to make a change. Find something daring to do every day, every week, every month—whatever fits into your schedule. Be daring with little things to build your confidence for the big moments. Always remember failure is positive as long as you allow it to be your teacher instead of your nemesis, while using it as a stepping stone to success. If you've been sitting on the sidelines, paralyzed by fear, you have the power within to turn things around instantly. There's no reason to watch everybody else have all the fun.

In the *Dos Equis* beer commercial campaign the main character is *The Most Interesting Man in the*

*World.* He's a gentleman of class and distinction, full of wisdom and charm. In one of the commercials the commentator says about him, *"He once had an awkward moment, just to see how it feels."* Ultimately that's the type of confidence and comfort level you'll need to be daring enough to realize your Dynamic Destiny. Ideally there cannot be any awkward moments, only experiences from which you live and learn. Just get out there, get your groove on and *live in the power zone.*

One last question: *What dare will you come face to face with, that is your ultimate challenge, which will lead you to the realization of your Dynamic Destiny?*

# DELIVERANCE

*Are you able to deliver the goods, at crunch time, when everything is on the line?*

*Ultimately you will be judged by how you perform under intense pressure and how you finish the job. It's time to rise to the occasion and bring home the goods!*

*W*e've come a long way through the maze of the *Dynamic Destiny Principle*. We've ventured to *dream* with passionate *desire*. We've made unwavering *decisions* with faithful *devotion*. We've maintained fearless *determination* with obedient *discipline*. Above all, we've been *daring*. Now it's time for the bottom line—*it's time to deliver*.

Michael Jordan was the top dog regarding deliverance in his heyday. When everything was on the line—when it was time to put up or shut up—when it was do or die—what did he do? He simply raised his game to a higher level. He saved the day countless times with his heroic play. In one NBA Championship game against the Utah Jazz, everything came down to the final seconds and the Bulls had one last shot. As usual, the ball was put in Michael's hands to deliver the coup de grâce and hang another championship banner in the rafters of Chicago Stadium. Michael instinctively drove to the basket to attack the hoop and initiate contact, but he surprisingly stopped on a dime near the foul line. As he gracefully elevated into the air for one of his patented jump shots, time stood still. The question was *could he deliver again?* As you may have guessed or witnessed, the ball delicately went in the basket and the crowd went berserk. He hit the last shot, in the last game of the season, in the NBA Championship and walked off the floor a winner. It was the perfect end to another glorious season. For some reason he had what was necessary to become bigger, stronger and better when everything was on the line. Michael's genius delivered six NBA Championships to the Chicago Bulls and he's now regarded as the greatest basketball player of all time.

Legendary tennis player Monica Seles was a master of deliverance. Once she was playing in the French Open, one point from being totally beat down. It would have been a crushing defeat, but when most players play it safe in a tense moment because there is no margin for error, she became more aggressive—*even animalistic*—and she went to work. She transformed from a human being into something superhuman, and she did it time after time after time. In her mind she was probably thinking *I can always come back and gut out a victory...let's get it on!* Well, Monica got it on and pulled out the match, completing another glorious comeback. Undoubtedly, if you were backed into a corner in any type of competition, you'd want Monica Seles to have your back. Whenever I'm on the tennis court and it's a tight match I think *what would Monica do?*

Her tenacity and ability to rise to the occasion on the world's biggest stage put her in position to deliver nine grand slam tennis tournaments to her legion of fans around the world. She is surely one of the greatest athletes of all time.

Bill Gates, Microsoft founder, is one of the wealthiest individuals in America. During an interview about five years ago he spoke of his vision for the personal computer when he started Microsoft in 1975. At that time he wanted a personal computer to be on everyone's desk. In the industrialized world that vision has quickly come into reality; and because of Bill's extraordinary sagacity, combined with remarkable business acumen, Microsoft products are probably the most ubiquitous in the world. However, being the trailblazer that he is, Bill has since changed his position and is just as ambitious as ever. He now believes a computer should be in everyone's hand. Something tells me that mission will be accomplished and it's a sure bet he won't be on the sidelines watching somebody else bring it to fruition. It would be no surprise to see him in the middle of all the action giving directions and making it happen. Because he's able to consistently deliver high quality products to consumers across the globe,

Bill Gates has risen to an estimated net worth of over forty billion dollars.

Greg Louganis, Olympic springboard diver, was also a master of deliverance. Once during a competition he was on the 30 meter platform poised to deliver one of his many remarkable dives. He adroitly leapt into the air and began twisting and turning as he had done many times. However, as he came down to dive into the pool, he hit his head on the diving board and crashed into the water. Everyone was in utter shock thinking he may have broken his neck, but he calmly got out of the pool, climbed right back up on the platform, and positioned himself for another dive. Thousands of people held their breath as you could hear a pin drop. Everyone was thinking how in the world could he rebound from a complete catastrophe, which could have paralyzed him, only moments ago? Could he possibly block that out of his mind and rise to the occasion? As Greg placidly stood on the diving board he put himself completely in the moment. It was clear that whatever happened on the previous dive was erased from his memory banks. As he again leapt into the air, twisting and turning, he started to come down as everyone nervously watched; but, this time his head barely missed the diving board and he executed the dive with sublime perfection. It was unbelievable and without a doubt one of the greatest comebacks ever. Greg Louganis went on to win Olympic gold in 1984 and 1988, all because he could deliver at crunch time.

Essentially everything we've talked about in the previous chapters was just to get you to the point where you can rise to the occasion and get the job done. Whether we like it or not, we live in a bottom line world and the real deal is can you seal the deal and bring home the prize? No one cares about how hard you try. No one cares about how much time or money you spend. No one gives a doggone about how much blood, sweat and tears you invest. If you can't deliver when it really counts, you're up the creek without a paddle. In our society success is all about delivering, whether you sink the winning putt in a golf tournament or deliver the product to the consumer faster and better.

What it is that makes some people come alive and thrive, while others nosedive, when the heat is turned up? There are a lot of convoluted theories out there, but sometimes the answer is simply the obvious—*it's all about comfort level.* Maybe you were expecting some esoteric explanation, but some people are just comfortable under pressure and they live for the moment. Maybe their blood pressure is lower than normal or their pulse rate gets suspended in time, but regardless, on a hot summer day they're just as cool as the other side of the pillow. They rise to the occasion and make things happen.

It seems that some people are born cool while others acquire cool. If you're like me you were not born with it and you've probably choked on way too many occasions. You just didn't have *it*, whatever *it* is, when you burst out of the womb. If that's the case, you're left with no other choice but to acquire *it*. I've found the simplest way to acquire *cool* so you may deliver is to put yourself in the *pressure cooker*. Simply inject yourself into pressure situations, over and over again, which compel you to rise to the occasion. You may not be able to bring home the bacon in beginning, but don't be too concerned about it; and if you choke, so be it. The main objective is getting comfortable in the heat of battle. If you inject yourself into tense situations enough times you will eventually become comfortable under the gun and you'll start to perform at a high level.

Warren Buffet doesn't succeed in every business venture, does he? Michael Jordan missed plenty of shots, didn't he? But I'd bet my last nickel they're as cool as ice when the pressure is on. Sure, their adrenaline is sky high and they're probably nervous, but not to the point where they can't execute—*and it's all about execution.* They're comfortable in tight situations because they've been there so many times. Hall of fame tennis player Boris Becker once felt that Centre Court at Wimbledon was his playground. He didn't win every match on the most famous tennis court in the world, but he won his fair share of three Wimbledon titles through comfort and execution.

The average person won't put himself in pressure-filled situations. He will just settle for what's before him, never really daring to question *what if?* Hence, he never gets practice delivering under pressure and has greater tendency to choke. If you've ever listened to sports broadcasters they always rate *experience* as a major factor when it comes to winning or losing. The team with the most experience has a greater chance of *not* blowing the lead or a greater chance of making the heroic comeback. That's only because of the obvious—pressure is familiar territory to the experienced team. That being said, you must continue to stretch and put yourself in *unfamiliar* pressure situations until they become *familiar* to you.

Tiger Woods was once interviewed after winning a pressure-filled golf tournament. As he came down the final stretch, there was no margin for error and he thought *I kept telling myself I've been in this situation before and succeeded...I know I can do it...I just have to go out there and execute.*

In the process of going from *unfamiliar* to *familiar* pressure situations, you must also be *prepared* to ascend to a higher level of performance. Going back to Michael Jordan, whenever he was on the foul line near the end of a close game, he rarely missed a foul shot. He was never the best foul shooter in the NBA, but when the pressure was on, he was the man you'd want to have on the foul line. His shooting stroke was always fluid and there never seemed to be a kink in his armor, yet there was no magic to it. He probably shot a couple of zillion foul shots to the point where he could do it blindfolded. As a matter of fact, Michael once made a foul shot against the New York Knicks with his eyes closed. Obviously we can't underestimate the value of practice.

Somebody one said practice makes perfect. Whatever you do, don't fall for that one. I know from practicing my golf swing that ain't nowhere near the truth. If you practice as hard as you can, but you're practicing the wrong things, *practice makes putrid* and you'll just stink up the whole place. Michael Jordan, like many top athletes, was disciplined enough to practice the proper things. He probably realized long ago that *perfect practice makes perfect*. With that philosophy Michael mastered the fundamentals of the foul shot, developed superior technique and ingrained good habits.

To deliver it's critical to understand the *power of positive habits*. We all tend to revert to our dominant habits when the pressure is on. In tight situations, when your nerves begin to rage uncontrollably, your mind can short-circuit. Something quirky happens and you may begin to do things that you are totally unaware of which come natural to you. If what comes natural is negative—*as in poor fundamentals or inferior technique*—you may as well take your ball and cry all the way home when it comes time to deliver. What you need is a guarantee that what comes natural to you is positive which will only happen through *perfect practice*. Through relentless repetition of the proper fundamentals you will eventually develop superior technique and a high level of skill which is infused and embedded into your subconscious. Then, when you're under pressure and your mind short-circuits, your subconscious takes over and what comes natural is positive. That's why Michael Jordan was so cool and he rarely missed a foul shot when everything was on the line.

Trumpet master Wynton Marsalis knows a thing or two about fundamentals and positive habits. Being a fellow trumpeter I'm always amazed by what he is able to do with his instrument. There seems to be nothing musically he can't execute and deliver, in front of a live audience, with dexterity and artistry. It's all because he knows what to practice and how to practice, which is the epitome of *perfect practice makes perfect.*

One of the greatest musical performances I've ever had the pleasure to witness was Wynton playing with the late legendary jazz drummer Elvin Jones. I was so spiritually moved by the music I had to go back the next night, with a different date, and hear the performance all over again. Wynton made it crystal clear that discipline and diligence is critical, while at the same time working on the right things, in the right way, at the right time. That philosophy has granted him the freedom to get more out of his instrument because he has fewer physical and/or mental constraints. Basically he can just let it flow and make musical magic. And to make it a little sweeter, he can play classical music equally as well as jazz, an accomplishment previously unheard of in the world of music. Pound-for-pound, through perfect practice, he's the best trumpet player in the world.

Additionally, when your fundamentals and habits are sound, combined with God-given talent, a positive mental attitude and, most important, a superior work ethic, you can elevate yourself into elite status. What separates the likes of Michael Jordan, Wynton Marsalis and other elite artists from the great performers in their respective fields is that they *vacillate at a higher level.*

During any particular performance anyone could have a good or bad day, and no two performances are exactly the same; therefore, we often look at the average performance as a barometer of greatness. On a given night a great performer may vacillate between levels 7 through 10, but an elite performer may vacillate between levels 9 through 10. Of course, that boosts the elite average performance to a higher level of 9.5, with the great performer averaging 8.5. That may not sound like a big difference, but it's all the difference in the world when you're engaged in heated battle. The advantage of being minutely better should never be underestimated. When Tiger Woods dominated the golfing world his average score per round was only about half a stroke better than his competition. When a world class racehorse wins by a nose it's only a millisecond faster than the runner up. Make no mistake about it, the magnitude of being *slightly* superior puts you in position to thrive when the pressure is on. Most important, it gives you the winning edge and creates champions. But, it all begins with mastering the fundamentals and developing good habits.

Another key when going from *unfamiliar* to *familiar* pressure is adjusting your attitude about the situations you're in. Sometimes it's as easy as asking a few simple questions. To start off, *what if I tried one more time?* It's amazing how many times you can deliver with one last ditch attempt. You build your confidence, get a few successes under your belt, and then the *unfamiliar* becomes *familiar*.

*What if I did it differently?* I'm embarrassed to admit how many times I've done the same things over and over and expected different results—and by the way, that's been said to be the definition of insanity. Sometimes you've got to mix it up to deliver.

*What if I got some help?* I can't tell you how many times I was unable to deliver simply because I was a hard-head and I wanted to do it my way. There were too many times to count when my way was the wrong way. Don't get me wrong, Frank Sinatra's rendition of *My Way* is a classic, but sometimes you have to do it someone else's way to get the job done. Don't think of it as being a copycat, think of it as not being an idiot trying to reinvent the wheel. Some people have already perfected a system and it is there for you to take advantage of. When necessary tweak it to make it suit your needs.

Also doing it someone else's way could be by getting a coach. Never be afraid to ask for help. All of the greatest athletes have a coach. There are also business coaches who advise corporate executives and entrepreneurs. If you can't find a way to get the job done, somebody who can see the job objectively can be your greatest asset. That person can make major or minor changes to your method and put you in prime position to deliver every time.

Regardless of how big and bad you may be you need help to rise to a higher level and deliver, just like everyone else. The way to rise high is to ask the right questions. Throughout our time together I've asked many questions of you for a specific reason: *questions compel you to focus.* By adjusting and fine-tuning your focus there's no telling how much more you'll be able to deliver when it counts.

What immediately needs fine-tuning is what questions we ask ourselves. Whenever you ask a question of yourself your focus shifts and you immediately start searching for an answer to the question. The weird thing is you will normally get an answer for your question, even if it's the wrong answer. Your mind is thirsting for something to work with, so in the absence of good answers it will run with bad answers.

For example: *How come I always keep failing?* I used to ask myself that question all the time. When I didn't know the reason why, the answer I came up with was *Kirk, you're a loser, that's why.* Of course, that answer blows your self-esteem right out of the water. Then, through proper training, I learned to ask myself empowering questions. For instance: *How can I get the job done? Who do I know who can help me? What would happen if I did A, B, C instead of X, Y, Z?* Immediately my mind searched for answers which started a chain reaction of events. Those chain reactions have led me to the deliverance of the ultimate successes I've had in my life and putting this book in your hands so we may share ideas.

Here's a simple question for you to ask yourself: *Can I do it?* Good question, right? Wrong! That's an ugly question because the phrase *Can I* could bring a serious amount of doubt to the table. The most popular answer is *no, I can't,* a self-defeating conclusion far too many of us have deeply rooted in our psyches. If that answer pops into your head and you embrace it, you've crashed head first into a brick wall with little chance of recovery. My best guess is that if you start a question with *Can I* you have a 90% chance of failure. So rule number one is to stop asking questions that start with *Can I* and replace that pathetic phrase with *How will I. How will I do it* is a lot more powerful, isn't it? I'd wager my last pair of shoes the 90% chance of failure with *can I* turns into a 90% probability of success with *how will I.*

The answer to *How will I* questions always produces a variation of two responses, both of which are positive. The first response is *I will do A, B, C,* which ain't a bad response at all. It shows you have confidence and focus. It also shows you're prepared to commit to a certain course of action, even if that course is not the right one. The bottom line is you have something to work with which is always a good thing.

The second response to a *How will I* question is *I don't know.* Whatever you do, don't fear the *I don't know* response. There's absolutely nothing negative about it's often the most lucid and powerful response you will ever have. Many people won't admit they don't have the answers and that causes major chaos in their lives. Oftentimes they will concoct an answer, just for the sake of having one, to cover up their ignorance. Some take it even further and become an obnoxious know-it-all. Those types of folks always remind me of something I heard years ago: *It's not what you don't know that gets you into trouble, it's what you think you know that ain't so.*

The power and beauty of the *I don't know* response is that it can compel you to *find* and *create* opportunity where it presently may not exist. When you truly want to succeed admitting *I don't know* opens your mind and allows light to cascade in through the prism of your consciousness. *How will I* questions and *I don't know* responses ultimately put you in a *seek and ye shall find* mentality. Without question it is and will always be your most potent state of mind.

It exponentially increases your probability of success by guiding you to some entity or someone who does have the right answers. That entity or someone may become a powerful ally who may open doors for you that you would never be able to open for yourself. All you have to do is flip *I don't know* into *who does know* and things will start to happen. Of course, *How will I* questions don't guarantee success, but at the very least they give you a fighting chance. Sometimes that's all you need to deliver the goods.

Let's look at a scenario to see how a chain reaction might work. Questions: *How will I make things happen? How will I deliver? How will I get the job done?* Personally the job I wanted to get done was to become a motivational speaker and syndicated columnist. I figured the first thing I had to do was put myself in take-off position. I had no major successes in my life, I didn't have any money, nor did I have a family name to open any doors for me. In the eyes of the world I was basically a nobody.

Once I was heartbroken when I first started out by a friend who said to me, in the most cynical and sarcastic tone, *"Why would anybody want to listen to you?"* At the time it hurt, but then I thought about it and she was right, why would anybody want to listen to me? I had a lot of dreams and desires, but did that mean anything? Regardless, I'd always believed there was something special and powerful deep within me and all I had to do was find a way to bring my gifts to the surface so I could live my dreams. In the eyes of certain people you may be a *nobody*, but in the eyes of the Almighty you're the greatest thing since sliced bread—*don't forget that fact.* So, for future reference, if you're ever reminded of your *nobody* status by friends, family or other unenlightened individuals, don't let those people break your spirit. They're simply hurdles for you to jump over and leave in the dust.

To get over my *nobody* status another question was invoked: *What can I do which doesn't cost me a dollar?* Being flat broke at the time that was an obvious question. I thought, of course, I can write a book or write articles to gain notoriety because being published is undoubtedly a great asset. I immediately looked for publications I could write for and I got an assignment as a motivational columnist for a national magazine. It had a small circulation, but it was the perfect start.

Then I thought *why not write a book and turn it into a CD?* All I needed was a computer and some software, which wouldn't cost a ton of money. I'll produce the manuscript and I'll do all of the recording at home. Then I'll let some people who understand the publication industry read the manuscript and listen to the CD. Tweak it here, tweak it there, and I'd have a finished product to sell.

*How will I publish and distribute it?* Having friends in the magazine industry I knew distribution was a major issue. Anybody can write a book, but making it available for public consumption is a completely different ballgame. But, thanks to the internet, the landscape of the publishing and distribution businesses is vastly different than it was years ago. Since I was a new kid on the block it would be a long shot to have one of the big publishing houses welcome me with open arms, so I could self-publish and distribute over the internet. I could have a website built and reach people all over the world.

It's easy to see how asking the right questions works—*it simply ignites a chain reaction.* One question leads to another and another and another, until eventually you bump into the right answer and stumble into success. Even if you ask dumb questions and get silly answers, your mind opens up and becomes receptive to unlimited possibilities. With repetition eventually you'll start to ask powerful questions and powerful answers will be returned. Believe it or not, when you start asking you will start receiving—*and then you'll start delivering.*

Deliverance is the icing on the cake of the *Dynamic Destiny Principle*. Therefore continue to put yourself in those pressure filled situations until they become familiar and your comfort level increases. Get away from *Can I* and start thinking *How will I*. Remember, there is no magic to delivering and it ain't nuclear physics. You just have to go about it the right way.

In the introduction I mentioned a quote which takes us from *sowing a thought* to *reaping a destiny* (*page 7*). At this time that quote deserves an enhancement. Sometimes we must tweak things a little bit to make it fit our circumstances and bring it to life. Let's test a new first line and see what happens...

> *If you sow a **How will I** question, you reap a thought...*
> *If you sow a thought, you reap an action...*
> *If you sow an action, you reap a habit...*
> *If you sow a habit, you reap a character...*
> *And if you sow a character, you reap a destiny.*

In closing, there is a very special concept we must take note of. In the chapter on *Daring* we spoke about *The Most Interesting Man in the World,* champion of the *Dos Equis* beer commercial campaign. He lives a life of intrigue and passion that most would love to capture. Unfortunately far too many of us are enviously watching other people deliver, maybe even jealously, while wishing we could have an inkling of their successes to experience the thrill of it all. Obviously that ain't happenin'— *you've gotta live your life.* But the real deal is that *The Most Interesting Man in the World* has accomplished the ultimate feat. As the commercial commentator says, *"He lives vicariously through himself."* He's not coveting another person's success. He creates his own adventure. He's comfortable in his own skin. He's not a prisoner of the past, nor is he a slave of the future—*he lives for and thrives in the moment.*

Once you get a taste of living in the power zone and bringing to life your Dynamic Destiny you will pass a point of no return. There will be no going back to the old you and your days of complacency will cease to exist. As one of my former college professors would say, you will be gratified, but never satisfied. You'll want more because you'll be able to deliver more. You may even develop an obsession with delivering for yourself and those you cherish. Don't fear it; take it and run with it. As you're running don't be surprised when you start living vicariously through yourself. The world will be your oyster, you will engage in your own exhilarating adventures and you'll have a heckuva lot of fun. I congratulate you in advance!

Your day to deliver is here and now and your Dynamic Destiny is calling—*can you hear it?* All you must do is ***Live in the Power Zone.***

# EPILOGUE

*It's your life...Live in the Power Zone!*

*A*t this point there should be nothing holding you back, nor should there be anything blocking your path of success. If you feel as though you're caught between a rock and a hard place, it is most likely due to a series of self-imposed limitations which have you mentally chained to a post. You can and you must break the chain. Only by doing so will you liberate your spirit, *live in the power zone* and benefit from your full potential.

As you should, you probably expect great things from yourself. You know you can attain any goal you set and it's simply the six inches between your ears which will determine your fate. You now have empowering Dynamic Destiny concepts for dreams, desires, decisions, devotion, determination, discipline, daring and deliverance. Essentially you have everything it takes. You're only requirement is to bring mental prowess to the table to get the ball rolling in the right direction; nevertheless, at this time, a few final thoughts.

Let's revisit the first Dynamic Destiny concept of dreaming. When you believe, feel and act on your dream you'll face some of the toughest challenges of your life. You may give everything you have, while going above and beyond the call of duty, yet that may not be enough to get the job done. You may be ridiculed by family and friends, as you pick yourself up off the ground after taking a big tumble. You may be brought to tears, as you agonize through failure after failure, before you get the slightest hint of success. Worst of all you may feel abandoned. During those moments don't be surprised if you find yourself staring in the mirror as you contemplate quitting and crawling under a rock. Why does life work like that? Sorry to answer a question with a question, but, *who knows?* I have no clue and I've never heard a good answer to that question, except as my grandfather would say, *"It is what it is."* As that is the truth, your ultimate challenge is to keep your mind and spirit free to allow divine intervention to work in your favor. You must be faithful enough to trust in things that cannot be proven and defy the intelligent man's sensibility. Frankly, some things just don't make any sense at all, but some of those things that don't make any sense can empower you beyond belief.

Throughout these printed words we've discussed many different ways to influence your Dynamic Destiny; but, to be honest, sometimes you need a miracle. Okay, maybe miracles don't exist since they can't be proven—*but who cares?* Call it divine intervention, luck, fate, synchronicity or serendipity, but it all boils down to the same thing: *something you did not make happen, which some ineffable force did make happen, that worked out in your favor.*

For instance, how can you explain how two people met at the exact time they needed to? Each struggled to get by independently, but they bumped into each other at the convenience store, started a conversation and their collaboration produced incredible results. Had they not been thirsting for a quart of orange juice at the same exact time, they may never have crossed paths. It can't be explained and in a sense it is a miracle. Suffice it to say you must do everything humanly possible to get the job done and let the Almighty take care of the miracles, but those miracles will only happen with extreme belief, hard work and, most of all, good karma. Take my word for it that everything you do comes back to you— *good and bad.*

You've been asked to be daring and take risks. Whether you realize it or not, life itself is a risky proposition. When you burst upon the scene, fresh out of the womb, you took the biggest risk of your life by taking your first breath, which was indeed a miracle. If you had played it safe at that moment you wouldn't be playing at all. Therefore, you can and you must continue taking risks, not by rolling dice in Las Vegas, but by putting faith in all the gifts you've been endowed with and taking ambitious action with them. Over the years I've come to agree with the great American writer Erica Jong who believed, *"The trouble is, if you don't risk anything, you risk even more."* With that thought in mind it's never too late to risk the first step toward your greatness. As the late, great jazz genius Charlie Parker told us, through the euphony of his saxophone, *Now's the Time*.

There was a movie entitled *Miracle at St. Anna* where in the final scene a gentleman said, *"Safety is the greatest risk of all because safety leaves no room for miracles...and miracles are the only sure things in life."* Since you only have one life to live and you may never come this way again, why not embrace the miracle of life itself and enjoy the journey.

In the process I have one last challenge for you. At approximately 2:00 a.m., after a beautiful Christmas Day in 2009, I could not sleep so I turned on the television. Luckily I caught *The Oprah Winfrey Show*. As usual Oprah was delivering at a high level and the topic was what we can do to help those less fortunate around the world. There was an organization being featured which said with just $27.00 per month you can completely change the life of an abused woman in the Congo Republic. Many ladies there were subject to genocide and other unimaginable atrocities and they would greatly appreciate any help. Of course, $27.00 seems like a miniscule amount, but for someone on the other side of the world it can make all the difference in the world.

Therefore, in pursuit of your Dynamic Destiny, your challenge is to *be a miracle* for someone else and *pay it forward*. To be a miracle doesn't take much and it doesn't matter how you do it, you just have to get the ball rolling. Simply release something positive into the universe others can feed off of, then wait and see. Who knows, you may make someone's dream come true. You may inspire someone to inspire someone else, and the chain reaction produces all types of wondrous results. And the more seeds of positivity you sow along your journey, the greater the quality of your life. By now it's blindingly obvious you're going to realize your Dynamic Destiny. The only question is who else can you take along for the ride? Let's make it happen. **Live in the Power Zone.**

www.ingramcontent.com/pod-product-compliance
Lightning Source LLC
Chambersburg PA
CBHW061432040426
42450CB00007B/1012